THE BIG BOOK OF LOVE

Loving Yourself, Dating With Love, Loving Relationships

By Jo Warwick

Copyright © 2016 by Joanna F Warwick

All rights reserved. This book or any portion thereof may not be reproduced or used in any manner whatsoever without the express written permission of the publisher except for the use of brief quotations in a book review.

ISBN: 978-0-9956607-5-5 (Print)

Published in the United Kingdom Cover Design by CRJ Design www.jowarwick.com

In LOVE for the Light that guides me…

Table of Contents

About Jo Warwick ix

Introduction xv

How Abuse Led Me To Love xvii

PART 1: LEARNING TO LOVE YOURSELF 1

Part One Introduction: Learning To Love
      Yourself 2

Chapter 1: 10 Reasons To Remember Why You're
      Loveable 5

Chapter 2: Why Emotions Are Your Greatest
      Strength 9

Chapter 3: The Ebb And Flow Of Love 15

Chapter 4: Find Yourself Again 23

Chapter 5: How To Embrace Change 41

Chapter 6: Directions To Happiness 47

Chapter 7: 11 Essentials To Becoming A Confident
      Happy Adult 57

Chapter 8: How Trust Can Transform Your Life 71

Chapter 9: Why Patience Really Is A Virtue 79

Chapter 10: Discovering Your Place In The World 85

Chapter 11: Embracing Your Passion 91

Chapter 12: The Masculine And Feminine Blueprint ... 97

Chapter 13: 10 Priceless Life Lessons 105

Chapter 14: Letter To Your 13 Year Old Self 111

PART 2: DATING WITH LOVE 113

Part Two Introduction: Dating With Love 114

Chapter 15: Why Loving Is A Choice But Love Isn't ... 117

Chapter 16: Why Do You Want A Relationship 121

Chapter 17: Are You Ready For Love Again 129

Chapter 18: 13 Mistakes Of Dating Without Love 135

Chapter 19: I Matter, You Matter, We Matter 149

Chapter 20: Bees Do It, Birds Do It, Lets Fall In Love, But Do You Know How 161

Chapter 21: 3 Ways To Improve Your Success In Love 169

Chapter 22: 18 Essentials To Dating With Love 175

Chapter 23: Bridging The Divide 185

Chapter 24; Love, Sex And Lovers 195

Chapter 25: Your Love And Life Assessment Questionnaire 203

PART 3: HEALTHY LOVING RELATIONSHIPS....207

Part Three Introduction: Healthy Loving
        Relationships 208

Chapter 26: Love Or A Pain Vibration.........................211

Chapter 27: Why People Blow Hot And Cold 219

Chapter 28: Confusing Being Serious And Committed
        With Love..227

Chapter 29: Why Communication Is So Much More
        Than Words 233

Chapter 30: Why Love Needs Space To Flourish........241

Chapter 31: Closer Friendships And Lovers................247

Chapter 32: 6 Ways To Keep A Love Connection In
        A Busy Life 253

Chapter 33: 8 Essentials For Keeping A Relationship
        Working...257

Chapter 34: The Miraculous Pull And Push Of Love... 263

Acknowledgements..273

About Jo Warwick

The Big Book Of Love is based on a collection of writing by Jo Warwick over the past ten years on her life's work; combining both her personal journey and professional experience and research.

Since 2006 she has worked with thousands of men and women in the UK, Ireland, Europe, USA, Canada and Australia, to understand and embrace Love.

Former professional sportswoman, born energy healer, turned writer and therapist (individuals, Couples, children and family), specialising in human attachment and the psychology of Love. She spent 15 years researching human development and relationship dynamics, as well as collecting miraculous love stories, during her global travels.

She's published on her specialism in professional journals, presented workshops, spoken at conferences and created an online self-help empowerment programme. As well as an avid traveller she's also spent many years in spiritual study and trained in Taoist Wingtsun, Yoga, Surfing, and Fencing, all of which has been integrated into her holistic philosophy and approach.

Testimonials

"Thank you for giving me confidence and hope and for showing me how good life can be once again." — Peter

"Jo the most amazing things are happening in my life! I am now walking toward those things that are good, light and safe for me! I have taken inspired action and now my path is being clearly laid out in front of me, So exciting" — Dina

"I have emerged as a stronger, wiser and more contented man. I now face the future with excitement, curiosity and love." — Mike

"Jo taught me about balance and negotiation within attracting and having a healthy relationship. About being happy within myself. Now that I nurture and care for myself first I see this reflected in my partner. What were problems and anxiety before are now new experiences and excitement for the future --I deserve them" — Mo

"I now feel love and give it freely; I can't explain how fantastically comfortable and enjoyable that feels. I am truly grateful to Jo for helping me." — Jonathan

"Jo has taught me that love really is patient, kind and unconditional. Firstly, teaching me how to love myself this way and that I deserve it and never settle for less. Secondly how to attract it into my life have that LOVE reflected. I have met a man who accepts me for who I am - flaws and all" — H

"Jo has helped me become better at loving my family and friends which has now given more than hope for the future. I am interested in life again and look forward to what is to come rather than being afraid. The sun now shines in my heart and I am so proud to have had the courage, to have been brave enough to find myself. I am so grateful for her help in bringing back to life again" — James

"I started dating again after a painful break up and Jo helped me realize that I didn't have to work so hard at it! I simply had to make sure I was fully being myself – with all my passions, likes/dislikes, love, and creativity. The experience of being my strongest, fullest, quirkiest self and feeling even MORE desirable was an incredible feeling!" — Karen

www.jowarwick.com

Reader Reviews
For The 1st Edition Of The Big Book Of Love

5* Review: Life-Changing and Enlightening!
"This truly is a life-changing book and one of the best I've ever read. Packed with advice, inspiration and wisdom, as well as interesting anecdotes and thought-provoking questions, The Big Book Of Love will make you feel enlightened and empowered, no matter your age, gender, or relationship status.

I feel like a different person after reading Jo's masterpiece, someone who is more open to love and more accepting of myself and others, and now I'm able to transfer all that I have learned into my own life and personal relationships."

5* Review: Does what it says on the tin. So inspiring!
"Really beautiful book with excellent practical guidance to enable you to love with an open heart. A book I will return to time and time again. Much of it definitely resonated in terms of what real love wasn't. A must for all!"

5* Review: Remembering what Love Is... through this book.
"Absolutely loved Big Book of Love. It provided the reminder and the tips on how to be the place that loves show up, both within ourselves first and then with others. Jo writes in a way that is relatable, heartfelt and deeply meaningful. I love her and genuinely appreciated this piece of her work. Highly recommend!"

5* Review: It's wonderful for untangling our relationship with ourselves and others
"This book is written from the heart for the heart. It is wonderful for untangling our relationship with ourselves and others.The author is frank and honest with her own life lessons and this makes you feel really at ease. It has really helped me to find the love within myself which in turn has really helped my relationships on all levels. A wonderful book to help set you free from self doubt and fears."

Introduction

*"To love yourself is the truth, to love another is
a blessing, to be loved is your reflection"*

- Jo Warwick

We are naturally designed to learn about love and relationships from birth through demonstration, experience and then practice. However, so many of us have missed out on a healthy or complete education and so instead feel separated from LOVE, confused with what it really is and how to have a healthy loving relationship. Leaving us feeling lonely, unworthy and failures in what should be the most natural and wonderful experience of life.

The purpose of The Big Book Of Love is to remind you that you are love at your core and teach the truth and reconnect you with LOVE. Secondly to offer the right skills and tools to make practical Love based choices not only for your daily well-being and happiness but to attract and create truly intimate lasting relationships.

Although this is a book about love and relationships, it is focused on practical life skills with love as the foundation. Not with rules and game-playing, but through suggestions, exercises and 'how-to' education and a bit of psychology, as well as storytelling to resonate with your journey and guide you forward.

There may be things in the book you already know or have heard of before and some different approaches that you haven't. It is split into three sections and at the beginning of each you'll find an introduction on how to get the most out of it. Each part builds on the one before, so it's best to start at the beginning and allow it to guide you. You can always revisit sections later on.

The book is designed to work on many levels, including your subconscious and conscious thought, to provoke and irritate you out of the old beliefs and ways, educate and agitate you into action and inspire you to open to more love in your life, just they way Love does.

If you don't understand something in a chapter don't worry there is a process to the sections and repetitions throughout, as it takes several times for things to resonate. We only ever learn what we are ready to receive, so you'll probably discover that if you re-read it at a later date that there will be new things you did not register before.

You don't have to be single or avoid relationships whilst you begin to love yourself, but its best to give yourself plenty of space and YOU time. However, our interactions with others are essential to our growth and capacity to open up to love more.

Be kind and gentle to yourself though, you are changing the education of a lifetime and that takes bravery. Don't rush your way through, but try to enjoy the process of discovery.

Love Jo xxx

How Abuse Led Me to Love - My Story

14 years ago I was a healthy, slim, beautiful young woman yet I stood cowering in the corner of my boyfriend's bedroom, in the semi-dark, half-naked frantically putting my clothes on, desperate to not let him see me naked, so he wouldn't be repulsed!

It had barely taken 3 months in this relationship to lose myself and for my self-esteem to be on the floor. Yet in a moment of out of body clarity, I heard a voice in my head say: What the hell was I doing? How have I ended up here…again!

In my rock bottom moment in the bedroom, as I saw myself naked and afraid, I was inspired to say - ENOUGH! I have to make a change and learn how to have healthy relationships, so I can feel safe and loved!

I had been a magnet to dark and twisted souls and over and over, finding myself back in the victim role. Born with spiritual gifts of energy healing and sensitivity to others, and then experiencing sexual abuse as a child, I'd come to believe it was my fault that other people were unhappy and it was my job to make them better!

Armed with a plan I first trained as a relationship counsellor and then a psychotherapist. I was obsessed with learning about abuse, fear, love, and attachment. I was determined to get to the root of it all and have the solution to all my problems.

I racked up thousands of hours with clients, had years of therapy myself. For years safe in my 'heady' world, as the observer, seemly confident, yet I was lonely and desperately wanted mutual connection.

So I started dating and the pattern began again. As I attracted the same kind of man and relationship, over and over again and each time I would crumble again. I felt like such a failure. I was stuck in a pattern I couldn't seem to get out of.

It would take the next guy to finally reach breaking point; where I would finally see THE TRUTH.

My new level of rock bottom came as lay on the cold granite floor of the church doorway as I sobbed, begging for help and the strength to carry on. I choose that day not to die, but to hold onto life for my dog Faith and my parents!

All that time I had believed a relationship with a man would hold the answers…if only I knew how to have a relationship, how to make it work, how men thought - I would have control, be safe and finally be loved! I had been looking for Love in all the wrong places.

It was from here that I finally surrendered control and returned home to what I had been teaching my clients and knew through my gifts all long: what LOVE really is as energy and where LOVE actually comes from and that it is unconditional and available to all.

I had been armed with all this great new knowledge in my head, but unconsciously in my body and behaviour I was putting out the same old energy and beliefs that I was attracting back in my life; that I believed I was not only unworthy, but somehow BAD and worthless. I felt unsafe in being me!

I was finally ready to allow LOVE to Love me. To accept that I matter and my life matters to me! That I needed to build my own LOVE foundation in my body to be secure, in and out of relationships, but also to change my vibration so I could attract the secure relationship I desired.

Over the next 6 years, I became my best client and integrated my mind, body, and energy. I became my own lover and partner, who made me feel safe, protected and provided for, so I could allow LOVE into my life from others without fear. The more secure I became in the LOVE within me the more my life transformed into being rich with wonderful intimate relationships.

I never want another woman (or man) to be stuck in that horrific place of self-loathing, disconnected from love, wasting their beautiful life away on dramatic, painful and unloving relationships.

Which is why I wrote **The Big Book of Love** to offer a far smoother and quicker path to be guided back home to LOVE and healthy loving relationships.

Love Jo xx

PART 1: LEARNING TO LOVE YOURSELF

Part One Introduction: Learning To Love Yourself

"A person who is full of love is like a new fully pumped up tyre on a car. So that when you drive down a bumpy section of road the impact is minimal and when you are driving on a smooth road, you can drive faster, with ease and confidence..."

Loving ourselves is a life long relationship and experience. Learning how to do so though takes tools and skills that we may, or may not possess yet.

To shed all that is hiding us, from ourselves, through a gradual emerging process of letting go, surrender and forgiveness. Letting go of the guilt for being not what others thought we were, or for simply maturing and growing up to be independent. Forgiving our grief, the rage and resentment from past experiences, where we have felt 'not good enough or too much'. Then surrendering any fear we may have of who we really are and how powerful we can be, and how others may respond to that truth.

As we do this we slowly rediscover the beautiful truth within us all. Our full capacity and frailties which make up our strength, as we move into full possession of both the Yin & Yang. The masculine and feminine energy/characteristics/capabilities within us, no matter our gender or sexual preference and take complete ownership of ourselves and our lives.

Finally, we can grow out of being dependent/co-dependent with others, or fiercely independent, and instead begin to live in flow, balance and self-sustainability. Fully open to LOVE moving through us with ease, as we continually receive, connect and share with others and live in abundant joy, peace, happiness.

Part one of this book covers the essentials of 'I Matter ', because loving ourselves is the foundation of all love in lives. Without it we cannot truly know how to Love another and have healthy relationships.

The approach to learning to love yourself is holistic so the chapters focus on the practical, physical, spiritual and emotional elements of your being, no matter whether you're male or female.

We will look at what love truly is and the process of change using love. Why we need to receive abundantly and how to make love-based choices and take action that feels in alignment with your heart, soul and well being.

It may take a little time to reeducate your mind and body on healthy self-love behaviour, as you will have to challenge any old hindering and unloving beliefs and memories, but love can heal anything, so take small steps, there is no need to rush, as it is a process of unfolding and growth. It is not about becoming perfectly balanced at all times. We do not need to be spiritually enlightened gurus, highly mentally evolved, or treat our bodies as sanctified temples. We are good enough and worthy of receiving and giving love now.

We do need though the tools, understanding and self-awareness to ebb and flow with love and harmony, the majority of the time. To be able to adjust ourselves as quickly as we can when we become off balance so that our choices and responses to life come from Love and respect.

Although you may have similar features and characteristics to others, you are the culmination of your biological make up, life experiences and soul which makes you totally unique. So no one else can tell you what is right or wrong for you, only you truly know who are. I can only offer directions to help you through your personal journey of discovering and falling in love with your life and opening up to the right relationship for you.

NB: I would suggest beginning a journal (in a book, not on a computer) to place all your thoughts, experiences, questions, emotions of this journey every day, as though you are talking to a best friend, as it will help you to process the experience, whilst you continue living day-to-day and get to know yourself.

Chapter 1:
10 Reasons To Remember Why You're Loveable

Sometimes you may forget and believe you're not good enough to love, but without realizing someone else already see's all the amazing things about you and why you are so loveable. Let this be a reminder of how truly magnificent you are, just because you're YOU.

Your Smile

I don't care if your teeth aren't perfectly straight or gleaming white. To me, when you smile and it reaches your eyes which twinkle with delight, you show me who you truly are, and by doing this you make me feel as though you really see me and you're offering me a little part of your heart.

Your Capacity To Love

Even though you have felt great pain and hurt and have at times wanted the world to just swallow you up to stop your heartbreak, and although you sometimes try your hardest to hide it, you just can't stop loving. It's who you are. Even though it may take you a little time, you always return to wanting to share love in your life.

Your Courage

You say you're scared, and sometimes the world seems too big. It can be such a struggle to get out of bed in the morning and you just want to curl up in a ball, but every day you somehow find the strength to carry on and face it with such courage. You take small steps to love those around you, care for yourself and find pleasure in the smallest things; these things all add up to greatness.

Your Creativity

You manage to express how you feel and who you are in so many wondrous ways, sometimes even without words. What astounds me though is your clever creativity to hide and avoid those things you are not ready for; it really does take such great skill. I wonder what you could do if you put all that skill and energy into doing what you do want?

How Playful You Truly Are

Although you may sometimes forget and need reminding now and then, I've seen you let your hair down. When you let yourself forget what others think, I watch you transform into the young girl or boy you once were, alight with laughter, teasing and silliness. Just give you the chance to spend time with a young child and you will be right beside them in make-believe, creating mystical lands with Lego in your princess dress, or wielding a hero's sword, or creating magic with a simple ball.

How You Never Get Bored With Learning

Every day you learn something new. It may only be something small, but where do you store all this information? Just when I don't think you could remember any more, you amaze me by learning to play the piano, taking up a martial art, learning to dance or speak a new language; anything that entertains you. You seem to get most excited when the challenge ahead is a little daunting.

Your Compassion

Even though you have been busy working hard and have been stressed at work, somehow when I least expect it, you reach out to help another person who may be struggling and in need. Not only do you donate your hard-earned money, but when your neighbour or friend is sad or wounded by grief, you give them your time and compassion by offering a cup of tea, a listening ear, or simply warm arms to comfort.

You Never Stop Growing

Although I sometimes see you struggle and want to resist the changing tides of life, I am truly amazed at how you learn to adapt and grow with each ebb and flow, to become a little stronger and more confident in who you are. Even though it may take a little while, you always choose to let go of who you were before and grow into who you are today.

Your Passion And Desire Are So Attractive

When all is said and done, I have to tell you how sexy you are: the way you use your whole body to feel the world around you and enjoy the small pleasures of each day. The way you express your soul and what you hold in your heart through your words, actions and energy. It gives me such joy to see you on fire and light up with your passion for living and being YOU.

Your Sense Of Humour Keeps You Sane

You can see the funny side of life and its ups and downs. You manage to make light of situations that could easily drive you mad. Sometimes negative things happen in your life, but somehow you shake them off and laugh your way through. Your laughter is infectious and lifts the mood of those around you, so they don't take themselves or life so seriously. Please never stop laughing or seeing the humour in the beautiful ridiculousness of life.

Chapter 2:
Why Emotions Are Your Greatest Strength

"Just get over it; don't be so sensitive. Toughen up. Grow a thicker skin" I have heard this advice so much over my life, but I've never seen it make anyone happy. Advised that sensitivity is a weakness, we toughen up with thicker skins to protect ourselves and end up just bottling everything up inside, pushing away how we feel (and our experience) and hoping it looks like we're strong, instead of being strong.

It's like trying to avoid our own shadow; believing it's gone because it's behind us. Totally visible though to anyone else who cares to look.

Instead of becoming stronger, this denying and rejecting behaviour makes us more susceptible to danger, more fearful and wary, resulting in confusion and un-happiness, because we have thrown away the information we actually need to survive and thrive.

The Rhino's Lesson

While I was volunteering in South Africa for an animal conversation charity, I found myself in close proximity to a wild rhino in the early hours of the morning. She was beautiful. With only a few feet between us, and little shrub to block her path, she did not seek to fight or flee; she just stood there.

Although rhinos are quite blind, they have other strong senses, including smell, hearing, taste, external touch, and instinctual felt sense (internal and external nervous systems). They have thick, layered, armoured skin that protects them from sharp, thorny bushes, but they are not insensitive and tough. In fact, their survival and ability to thrive is wholly dependent on their sensitivity.

She didn't run or charge, because she didn't feel I was a threat.

Sensitivity Is Power

Sensitivity means to be connected and fully aware of all our senses. Our bodies are descendants of mammals, so we're sensory beings. This means, like the rhino, we are designed to use sight, hearing, smell, taste, touch, and felt sense to navigate the world around us and survive, because we have an internal and external nervous system.

This sensory information to external stimulus creates an internal response to everything, including danger and safety, separation and connection, otherwise known as emotions. It is a fact: we're all emotional, male and female!

Unlike our animal cousins, though, we have an evolved conscious awareness of this emotional information, so they become defined as feelings—the language of emotions to which we attach judgment.

Instead of responding naturally and appropriately to this navigation system, we stress ourselves out, worry, shame, analyse, get embarrassed, get scared, get stuck, don't act, ignore, or do the total opposite of what our body tells us to do.

The rhino does not question the sensory information the brain collects, it just acts appropriately either by running away and avoiding the danger, or standing still to assess and inquire. Or, by running toward it, threatening with their full force of size, strength, weight, and their strong, sharp horn, not because they are bad-tempered, but because they must still protect their well-being, even though they are naturally shy, curious, and non-predatory.

Confusing Safety And Danger

Our brain continually processes sensory information to inform our responses to a situation or person by encouraging slowing down, moving toward or further away. Teaching us to ignore, shame, disregard, and disconnect from this emotional sensory information leaves us unarmed, unprotected, and unsafe. It's like being in conversation, but only talking, never listening, and assuming what the other person thinks and feels.

The result:

- We're unaware of danger, so we don't know how or when to protect ourselves.

- We're unaware or unsure if the people we choose to surround ourselves with love, accept, and respect us, or are out to harm, belittle, or control us.

- We lose the ability to know what is right for our happiness, peace, and love.

- Our brains rewire to associate fear and danger with safety, and love and kindness with danger and being unsafe, so we seek the wrong thing. This would be like the rhino ignoring her survival senses, walking up to a pack of lions, and saying, "Hey, I'm just as big as you, can I come hang out…"

How A War Zone Becomes Your Norm

This behaviour is most obvious in adults who experienced abusive childhoods. Or were parented inconsistently, or conditioned to be good girls and boys and shamed for expressing anger, desire, or tears. In these environments, a child absorbs the message *"Ignore how you truly feel and don't express it"*

If they accepted the sensory information they received, they would have had to accept that their home environment, where they needed to be cared, protected, and provided for to survive and thrive, actually felt unsafe and rejecting to live in.

It's unimaginable for a child to acknowledge that the parents or home, they love might not feel or be safe, even if they come to see a difference in other families. They learn not to respond appropriately, as it could result in possible physical danger, punishment and abandonment, so they adapt and disconnect from their feelings and desensitize, do as they are told, try to please to make it safer, and stop trusting themselves.

If they continue this behaviour into adulthood, they will keep seeking out the familiar—hurtful, disappointing, painful, unstable, rejecting, or even dangerous relationships and circumstances, to mirror the feelings of childhood.

Getting Emotionally Reconnected

I used to think women who cried were pathetic. I thought they should just get over it and pull themselves together, as this was how I saw my own vulnerability. No matter how much loss I experienced every feeling I had was buried away, unspoken, and unshared, branded as either a sign of weakness, as regards to crying, or unacceptable, if it was anger. I considered every other feeling bad and dangerous.

My exterior toughened up until I was cold and hard as a stone. I chose abusive lovers, friends, and bosses over and over again, even though when I met them all I had the same uncomfortable, sickening, withdrawn feelings. I just ignored them and believed I must be wrong; and I jumped into, at worst, dangerous and, at best, rejecting and unloving environments. I moved towards what felt bad and rejected what safe and loving.

Part of my self-discovery was learning to get out of my judgmental head and back into my body; trusting its natural ability to know my boundaries and how to protect myself, so I could begin to make the right choices for my health, well-being, and happiness. I sought people who showed me how to demonstrate my emotions openly and gave me permission to feel angry and cry. I came to understand my body's language, so, if I felt something, I got real and responded appropriately.

- If I felt happy and safe, I smiled.
- If I felt safe and laughed, I opened my mouth wide and laughed wholeheartedly from my belly.
- If someone tried to disrespect me, I called them on it or walked away.
- If I felt the desire to touch and be touch, I trusted my intuition.

No longer confused and distrusting of my sensitivity, I didn't need to waste my energy fighting and denying how I felt. I could now be open to love and intimacy, no longer terrified of it as dangerous, or afraid of rejection, because I felt safe in my ability to know and act on the truth. Finally listening to the whole conversation and all the information I was receiving, so that like the beautiful rhino I could own our greatest strength of all: our emotional instinct to navigate the wilderness and know who is part of my herd.

Chapter 3:
The Ebb And Flow Of Love

In this chapter, we have a first introduction to what love really is and understanding how it works and how we can get aligned with it to have love abundantly in all areas of our lives.

Trusting and moving with the flow of Love takes an internal shift of focus, from how things look, to how they feel. Firstly, to your experience of your environment at that moment - including being in the company of someone else and how it makes you feel. If it feels right/light/expansive/comfortable for you or not. Then secondly to observing (sometimes over time) if how it looks or sounds matches how it feels. Always being aware of your response to the information and acting accordingly.

This shifts us away from fear to a freedom-based life, in which you thrive with Love and joy in every aspect of your life. This can only be achieved through practice and from being in a balanced state of mind, body and emotions, which comes from loving ourselves.

Starting With You

When we're off balance (either anxious and dependent, or defensive and rejecting), our current perception of situations in our lives becomes manipulated. We stop being in the present, 'the now' and using all our senses and default back to our earliest experiences and perceptions of the world and the have ingrained programming in our mind and bodies, even if they were completely twisted.

As children, our primary focus shifts from our sense of feeling - to sight and sound, or vice a versa, depending on how secure and loved we feel because we are wholly dependent on others to feed us, take care of us and keep us safe and will do anything to make sure that happens. We cannot focus on feeling when we cannot change our environment as a child, so if we don't feel OK, we will focus on looking OK and pleasing others, so we get cared for.

We will always adapt to survive, however, we are then supposed to outgrow this and into self-sustainable adults independent from the need of others to parent us and thrive.

Self-sustainable means regularly loving ourselves in all ways, so we feel secure, balanced and loved with, or without the added benefits of other people's influences, so things can come and go without affecting our core self.

Imagine your house and all the electrical items in it. Without a source of power, they are just lifeless objects. Now some will have a battery source and some only work if plugged into the mains circuit.

We have both a mains connection and a backup battery source. It is our job to focus on allowing our battery power to be fully charged at all times by connecting to the mains and then having the battery for emergencies, when we temporarily disconnect ourselves.

If we don't learn to love and respond to our own needs first and get plugged into the mains, then we will always be drawing from our much-needed resources (battery power), to give to other people to make them seem happier, so they will reward us in some way. It will trigger natural responses of fear of lack and not being enough, because there isn't and we are giving to get.

When we are plugged into the abundance of energy/love etc. we then have a surplus to share with other people either in mutual exchange, like a 'barter system', instead of a 'working for an employer' system, or we able to freely gift without a fear of loss, because we know we have more than enough.

Whatever our previous experiences, we must learn to love and care for our own energy levels, so that our resources are at least 70% charged: by taking care of our basic needs such as rest, food, water, exercise, laughter, sleep, but also doing the things we enjoy and give us pleasure — do our own thing!

To thrive, we then need to go beyond ourselves for additional recognition and interaction from friends, work, lovers, for mutual affection, play, growth, achievements and challenges. To reflect the love we feel about ourselves inside and experience the love we want to share. This takes us to 100%, although this is not a fixed state, but a fluid one.

Ebb And Flow

Love energy moves in ebbs and flow like the tidal shifts, like the sea flows towards the beach and then flows towards itself, the same happens as the energy pushes and pulls us forward out into the world, our desires and towards other people, then pulls and us back to focus on the love within ourselves and taking care of us to build resources, so that we shift like the sands ideally between 75 - 90%, so there are no highs and lows, just small waves.

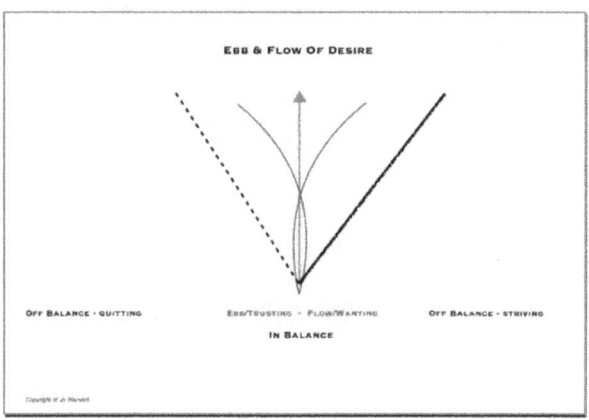

When we are focused on how things look we start to believe that there is only what my eyes can see, we have become off balance with depleted resources and begin to feel anxious and angry, we can either end up leaning forward and striving towards (as above), such as LOVE is only the thing or the person in front of me and without them I have nothing. The person - man or woman becomes an object or our only source of love.

If we have become off balance by depleted resources, we can also end up leaning back to far, into our inner fears, as though quitting/running away /avoiding from being in the present, feeling incapable.

In truth, though the whole world is energy and love is energy and everything around us is like a gigantic bank of love and the things that are manifested in physical form such as relationships are only a reflection of the part of the love we allow to flow through us. Not the sum of LOVE itself.

When we begin to see that we can have a relationship with Love itself as a whole force that flows through everything on the planet, instead of seeing it as something that is only given or taken by other people. We can gain perspective, lean back enough and relax into life, trusting in the unconditional flow, like floating in a river and then acting on inspiration and moving forward, so that move subtle between those to points (see image above)

Free Flowing

Every time we shift away from how it feels and our instinctual sense we fall back into how we perceive it, we put the brakes on to the abundant flow of LOVE. Like driving down the motorway and slamming the brakes on every 10 minutes!

If something or someone feels right it can come well in advance as an inner knowing, as though someone has turned on a light inside of you, even if it may take some time for the looking right and being manifested in the physical, which is why love takes trust and patience to allow it to unfold and fall into place.

No amount of something looking and sounding right (to an expectation or perception) will ever make it feel right, no matter how hard we try to make it so. Sometimes things that were right are no longer because they are only meant to be for an amount of time and act as a stepping stone - as the saying goes *"some for a season, some for a reason, some for a lifetime"*

Staying in the flow of LOVE and trusting in its guidance means if we feel attracted and it feels right: expansive/light/blissful/joyful and you feel seen and heard — move forward. If it feels wrong: dark/smaller/ restrictive/ chaotic with a sense of being jagged, sharp or as though you are being shouted at and you are fighting to be seen and heard then move away.

When we stay fixated on how it looks we cannot dream or create the life that we dream of. We just stay stuck attracting more fear, disappointment or able to move forward. We get frozen in fear that we don't have enough or what it takes to achieve or receive our dream.

When we surrender to the pull of attraction to what feels right and trust in LOVE to resolve all blockages our dreams and manifestations unfold with ease. It's like being a confident driver and having the motorway clear and spacious for you to cruise along and accelerate and overtake when you need to or want to.

Trust In Love

Being in the flow of the energy of LOVE means that like surfing when you catch a wave you have to learn the right moment to seize it, jump up and allow it to peel towards its destination. You cannot see where it is going. All you can do is learn how to feel the force of energy rise up, then paddle to catch up and ride the waves as it peels with you on it. Too late and you cannot follow it, as there will be no energy to take you. Rush and paddle too far ahead of it and you will be knocked over when the power of wave catches up with you.

So instead perfect your skills to listen, feel and be in harmony with the timing of love and how it moves and flows. Not only to catch a wave but to have the patience for the right wave to come. Then how to surrender and accept the full force of the wave and go with it, with total commitment to its final destination.

If it is the intention of the wave to peel all the way to the beach it will have enough force to get there. If though it is a shorter ride it will peter out after a short burst. You cannot make a short wave become a longer one; no amount of working it, pumping it, and fighting it will make its destination change.

Every wave comes to an end and recycles back into the ocean, so it is with LOVE. It never dies, it just recycles to begin again somewhere else. Once we know the rhythm and pattern of LOVE we can learn to practice to go with it instead of fighting against it.

We cannot change LOVE or the way it works and to try to do so exhausts us and wastes our lives. We can though learn to trust that instinctual knowing that something is right for us and if we feel the pull of love then ride it to its destination. Even though it may be scary and new and we don't understand why or how it will work out we can learn to go with it.

That is why to trust LOVE external to us we must first learn to trust the love which is internal, and our abilities to know what feels right or not. To trust ourselves to walk away, say no, or get out of the way of what doesn't feel right and to trust ourselves to step forward towards what is attracting us.

We can practice and test out our skills and like any surfer or driver when you start as a beginner and then with practice and time it gets easier and you make fewer mistakes and it becomes less conscious and more of a natural habit and you can begin to really trust yourself!

Just because you may not have in the past or at present been receiving the love you need or deserve, it can change so easily. The energy of Love is abundant and readily available outside and inside of you. All you have to be is willing to receive the guidance and act accordingly.

Chapter 4:
Find Yourself Again

Do you feel drained, bombarded or overwhelmed by the noise and negativity that seems to come from other people's complaints, problems, demands, opinions? The judgements distributed either via social media, advertising, TV, newspapers, in the office, or simply in your daily life from friends, neighbours, family or even in your relationship?

You don't have to just sit there feeling powerless to its onslaught. You can take action. You're allowed to take action. You're meant to take action against it and you don't have to feel guilty for it!

Take Action And Move Away

You're not weak for feeling this way, it's just you've become like a rabbit in the headlights. Accepting this behaviour from other people, including society into your personal space and not taking appropriate action to remedy the situation. Choose now to be empowered!

Minimise the amount of stress you have to deal with by firstly turning off and walking away from everything you can, as you don't need to keep adding to the load, so stop giving time to the obvious sources! Responding appropriately to your instinct and moving away from the causes of negativity, pain and stress, can bring immediate, a short term or long term remedy.

Too Much Crap!

Don't put up with emotional dumping from anyone including your 'friends', partner, family etc., because you're trying to be polite. This is not love, because you are not taking care of your well-being. Not caring for yourself and putting yourself last, helps no one! You're overwhelmed because there's too much emotional waste coming at you and your resources, energy and resilience have become depleted.

Fact - You cannot change other people!
Fact - You cannot make them see the truth!
Fact - You cannot make someone else alter their behaviour!
Fact - You cannot make someone else happy - only they can!

You can take care of yourself - build your resources, focus on your well-being, set boundaries by firstly moving away from the negativity and toxicity as much as possible and refocus your choices and attention towards love, joy, happiness, play, peace and what makes you feel good in the moment of each day.

Adults are supposed take full ownership of their lives by listening, accepting and processing how they feel and act on it. However, sometimes we can only come to that point when someone else sets the boundaries and says it's not OK to do that. Change your behaviour and those people in your life will have to acknowledge their own issues because you're not there doing it for them; well unless they find someone else who is willing to accept this behaviour.

It's Time To Replenish

It's time to retrieve some space and quiet to find yourself again and seek to replenish and calm your poor overworked nervous system, which is desperately trying to process the bombardment of stimulus that surrounds you!

- Turn off the TV and take a break from the drama, the soaps, the news, this can cause vicarious trauma - (secondary trauma) because we are powerless to change it.
- Shut the newspaper or stop buying it for a month (same reason as above)
- Turn off the music - or listen to music you find calming
- Turn off social media
- Turn off your phone
- Turn off PlayStations
- Get back to silence
- Or get outside into the soothing sounds of nature

- Go walking outdoors, by water, trees, on the beach
- Play with a pet
- Take some space to just breathe deeply and chill out safely
- Learn to meditate, do yoga etc.
- Have a massage

Why We Need Personal Space

Home is supposed to be a sanctuary from the outside world, a place where you can chill out, relax and have complete and utter downtime. Invite that bombardment from other people trying to get/take your attention in your home and you've instantly stopped your sanctuary!

Of course, we may live with other people, animals and so we can't always just walk away or shut the front door and hide away! So we have to learn to take more determined action, by setting personal boundaries to create personal space.

I overheard a woman in the shop the other day saying to her friend why she hated timeout for children and the other woman agreed as stating that her child was too sensitive to use a timeout. I found myself both curious and cross. As an observer, I noticed that the first woman seemed to ironically have a lack understanding of personal boundaries and space. She didn't leave room for the other woman to respond, even though she was asking questions. She was leaning forward into the other woman's physical space oblivious that she was leaning backwards trying to create more space.

Even more curious was that the mother of the so-called sensitive child was clearly uncomfortable, but she also didn't understand the importance of owning her personal boundaries. Although she was leaning back, it never occurred to her to move her feet backwards!

Timeout Is Not Punishment But A Life Skill On Taking Ownership

Over the years I have met so many adults who can't be alone in their own company because it feels so uncomfortable and consequently can't handle being single either. Being alone equates to being abandoned and punished, so to be alone or single means I must be bad. So relationships are then out of a fearful need, not love or desire!

Now I've often heard many parents say Time-Out doesn't work, but in further discussion, it becomes very clear that they are confused about its purpose and how they use it.

In the UK 1950s and earlier it was considered correct parenting to place baby outside in its pram in the backyard and leave it to cry so it would learn not to cry and be a 'good child'. The child does learn to stop crying, but it also learns to not trust those who care for it and to stop registering any emotions at all, out of pure terror of separation that it has been abandoned and left to die.

This is extreme, but for a lot of adults their fears of abandonment or uncomfortableness in being in their own company can be a result of being parented inconsistently and being sent to their room as punishment as a small child, isolated and with no clear definite end to the amount of separation time. Like being sent to prison without knowing your sentence or any chance of parole. This is often how people associate timeout. Their bedroom instead of being a safe space for relaxation is then associated with punishment and this treatment and experience becomes an internalised as an idea of home, personal space, and being — I must have done something bad.

The practice of Timeout is actually a tool for teaching a life skill. It is a way of gradually teaching your child to self-regulate their nervous system. Learn how to self soothe, calm down and cope with their feelings, [take responsibility] so they can begin to learn how to problem solve [take responsibility and take action]. To be able to take personal space and self-respect to live equally in a world full of other people.

Time Out Can Be A Life Saver

When time out is used as punishment; the child learns they only belong (and therefore loved) when nice, well behaved and compliant. Which results in teenagers and eventually adults who are both susceptible to control and domination from other people, predators and bullies, because they have little sense of personal boundaries, are afraid of their own power and will struggle to trust themselves and take action on their behalf to solve problems.

Time out is essential to our good mental, emotional and physical health. Taught as a life skill it creates adults who know who they are and how to respect themselves, their time and space and how they share it and who with! They know the benefits of 'Me' quiet time and see it as part of their daily life, which is essential for anyone living in our fast-paced hectic world,

Time Out For Tantrums

When we're distressed, angry and afraid, especially when we are in the stages of asserting our individuality as children and teenagers, we have tantrums. Honestly, though they can happen at any age if they've been emotionally repressed.

Tantrums are a build-up of emotional energy, which overrides the logical thinking part of the brain and is the equivalent of feeling like you're being chucked into a fire! It's normal and has an essential purpose and they can be scary, especially when we're very young. Part of our maturing is learning to experience the intensity of these feelings and energy, so we can understand them and master our emotional force to match our language appropriately and come into our power.

This can only happen though if we experience: *I am safe in my external environment, even though I feel unsafe inside*

That emotional energy is the power behind developing self-respect, sexual desire and attraction and being able to enforce personal space and boundaries, which allows us to have healthy, respectful relationships with other adults.

As the two women in the shop demonstrated in their lack of understanding and body language; if we don't know how to defend our personal space we get smothered and if we are not aware of personal boundaries, we smother other people.

Using Timeout With Children

When young children (up to 7) are behaving in a way that is not acceptable to you, say in very few words that this is not OK. Stop, give a warning of a timeout after the second clear statement. third time: timeout. Be calm, firm, simple and clear (don't shout).

If they begin to have a tantrum stay in the same area, don't leave, just step back a little keeping your child safe in a contained zone, but giving them space. Do not engage with them with verbal chat, physical contact, or eye contact as they are only expelling raging energy and cannot hear you. They're like a fire breathing dragon and you must be the castle walls; solid, secure, calm physical presence! Don't feed the fire, but be a calming presence.

Once they've calmed down enough then you use a dedicated area in the same room on the floor or bean bag, or a tree or a few feet away from you if you are out which is safe that they can go and sit to calm down completely and have some time to relax. Be very clear about the amount of time they will be there for - no more than 5 minutes for younger children and 10 minutes maximum for a child up to 7 years. Have a clock visible to them if you are at home.

It is very important that we don't demonstrate passive-aggressive behaviour and continue to be cross with them, it wasn't personal. Once they have calmed down they get lots of eye contact, smiles and hugs to reconnect with you which demonstrates they are still loved – unconditionally and can be forgiven for behaviour.

State the behaviour that was not acceptable, be very clear, simple and without judgement - *"I love you, but I don't like it when you do/behave ..."* Do not ask them why they did something or behaved a certain way; they don't know why, but they will try to make up reasons to make you happy.

Timeout is extremely effective when children/young people are overexcited/overstimulated, the same goes for adults, (and often this can be a precursor to a tantrum) so teach them how to go to their bedroom(safe place - leave the door open if they want) and listen to music, draw or read etc (not TV, Movies, Video Games or mobiles as these are stimulants) and have some 'alone downtime' and self soothe.

The earlier and consistently Timeout is introduced to a child, the easier for them to learn and be used effectively as a life skill and without resistance.

Using Timeout Can Save Adult Relationships

We all get pissed off and hurt, but that doesn't mean the relationship is over. It's just an argument and naturally part of any intimate relationships and it can be done healthily. Learning to give someone else, or take physical space and time to calm down, instead of losing complete control, can save a relationship because we stop acting out from fear and anger and say something we will not mean and regret.

As long as we make sure though, to reconnect again when you're both ready to talk more logically and responsibly, if perhaps still forcefully and emotionally until you can resolve the issue. Resolving the initial issue is the essential outcome, so use timeout as an opportunity to clarify your thoughts and feelings to express them clearly.

Never though use timeout as avoidance and for things to be unaddressed and brushed under the carpet as this teaches us nothing, but more avoidance and lying! So be honest and reconnect with physical love.

Taking Care Of You

Part of loving ourselves is learning how to respond appropriately to our needs with the correct natural response. We can learn how to create personal space, enjoy your own company begin to discover a sense of peace and override past experiences, but we need to learn a mixture of self-soothing, flight and flight activities to find our mental, emotional and physical balance and cope with life with ease. If we use the wrong activity we will stay imbalanced, overwhelmed, confused, anxious or angry and unsettled.

We are animals in our biological makeup and stress impacts our nervous systems. Some types of stress and lower levels can be highly beneficial, whilst others and high levels can be dangerous for our mental, physical, psychological sexual health. Most imbalances are caused by repressed historic emotional energy which makes us energetically constipated (blocked up) and unable to process the continued stimulus/stress we receive every day.

Test Yourself

Close your eyes for 60 seconds and place your left hand on your chest and then score yourself out of 1 - 10 how stressed do you feel?

1. We are supposed to live healthily in the 1 - 2 range with moments of alertness that would peak us up to 5 -6 we can return to peace. the lower our

natural functioning state the less affected we are by stimulants.

2. If our normal is 8-10 our nervous system is functioning and responding in survival mode, as though we are stuck in a war zone, or in trauma and it is essential we take immediate action! Also, make sure to have a health check with the doctor.

3. If we are in the higher levels of stress then we need to gently remove over two to three weeks, any stimulants from our diet, such as caffeine, alcohol and high levels of processed and natural sugar and social drugs, as well as visual stimulants such as computer games for 2-6 months, depending on what other stress we have in or lives from jobs, families and relationships and how well we use the exercises.

Calm Down - Self Soothing Techniques

We all need the skills and the time out of external life to self soothe and calm down. This taps into our nurturing and receptive feminine nature within us all and the aim is to feel safe. It takes at least 10 minutes to calm down, but when we are living at high-stress levels it can take months to calm down. Some techniques are useful for immediate remedy and some are ongoing care.

- In silence focus your whole attention on an object for 10 minutes, like a clock or the look at the sea or hills or your garden and only use that one.

- Sing or hum to yourself

- Take a warm bath – this is very calming to the nervous system

- Take twenty rounds of slow deep breaths - in through your nose and out through your mouth

- Listen to calming music or a meditation recording

- Let yourself have a good cry, this is the body's way of releasing toxins and healing

- Bake

- Paint or draw

- Massage your palms with your alternate thumb

- Read a book - not social magazines or online

- Watch calming movies - not violence.

- Meditate -in any way by being present in your body, not in your mind.

- Stroke a pet

- Stretching of your limb and back muscles

- Using an exercise foam roller, massage and release deep tissue toxins/stress every morning and evening(and after exercise) out of legs, back. Can be great for gently rolling on your tummy and releasing tension out of lower abdomen - repressed emotions often causing IBS.

Flight Based Activities

Sometimes we must take flight to create space we need; this is the flow of feminine energy (like water) The ultimate of flight is to leave things that feel bad and wrong for us, or simply take a break./holiday.

- Go walking (alone or with a dog)
- Run outside - grass, beach, park, track (not indoors)
- Dance anyway and anywhere you like
- Yoga
- Swimming

Fight Based Activities

Fight based activities help with assertiveness, releasing unexpressed rage and growth tantrums from the past and tap into our masculine, active nature so that we can take action with confidence in our lives and be able to protect ourselves and our personal boundaries.

So take time out to your blood pumping, get hot and get a sweat on. When we learn to do these things we can stop needing to repress our feelings or exploding/or fighting with other people because we are now taking charge and ownership of this force.

- Beat up your bed; Let yourself go fully and have a healthy tantrum in a safe place. Kneel on your bed with the duvet and pillow scrunched up in the middle, then raise a cushion/pillow over your head and then hit down on the pile has much as possible until your arms ache and you've had a good work out and released some tension. This is really powerful if you add shouting, swearing or growling and rageful music. Once completed open your windows and make your bed whilst breathing nice and slowly until you feel once again in control and you can see that you have tidied up any mess you've made, to feel in control.

- Stand upright, with your legs hip-width apart, if you can or in a chair if you can't. Then punch the air in front of you with both arms, until they grow tired, whilst shouting NO, or growling or swearing. Doing this to 'teenage rage- like music' can make this easier and fun!

- Scream, growl or swear as much as possible in your car - not at someone and ideally when stationary. make sure to open the windows when done to release the energy.

- Take up a combat sport/exercise such as boxing, martial arts, fencing, kickboxing.

- Scribble fiercely – express your pent up feelings that have no words.

- Team sports where you are physically competitive really help with this - hockey, football, rugby etc

Core Exercises

Also focusing on building our physical core strength and balance really helps with stabilising our sense of well being. It's not about looking good, but strong internal torso muscles, that act like the trunk on a tree. When we are physically weak this affects our sense of capability. A foam roller is great for facilitating core exercises.

Making Change To Finding Yourself

To feel confident, comfortable in our skin and able to cope with day to day life, we need to take time and find the perfect combination of the four sections above, not only to de-stress and rebalance but to continue to live with ourselves in harmony.

The percentages of each and which activities we choose needs to change depending on how high or low our constant stress level is - using the test.

Eg: a) If we are over-anxious then we need to do activates which firstly helps release the stress, calm us, then release the fight energy/emotional blockage, so that we can feel stronger.

b) If we are angry and stressed out then we need to self soothe and calm down, and then seek flight to create space and flow.

What may surprise you is that often we need to first relieve the initial reaction of the emotion we are aware of then - such as shout for anger, but then do an activity which is the opposite/counter-intuitive - such as run (flight).

It is the repressed emotional response underneath, which is the blockage and why we may take some action and not feel better because it is not the right solution to the problem. Until we take the appropriate response we won't rebalance. It takes practice, trial and error and play to discover which techniques work for you at what time, it cannot be prescribed, because it is about you getting to know yourself one step at a time.

Just remember the aim is to discover mental, emotional and physical balance — inner peace, confident, capable, healthy and happy, though your empowerment to take action on theses four essential things.

- Say no - in actions and words to anything that feels draining, heavy, uncomfortable or painful and remove it from your life, house or social life! Create space for yourself and personal boundaries.

- Build your resources and resilience and calm yourself down to get more comfortable in your skin. Use timeout and the Flight, Fight, Self Soothing and Core activities

- Always seek to move towards what feels good, pleasurable, comforting, light, spacious, peaceful, kind and loving. These equate as safe!

- Always move away from anything that feels overwhelmingly stressful, wrong, tiring, painful, blaming and shaming, dark, heavy and confusing.

It is important to not beat yourself up and get cross if you get a bit upset or distressed, instead understand that this is an opportunity to love yourself and develop your skills and self-trust.

When you become more comfortable with being in your own skin and in your personal space, then you will find it much easier to cope, be more emotionally literate and OK with your own company and be able to shake off negative stress with ease, although you will automatically allow less and less of it in your life.

Chapter 5:
How To Embrace Change

When we want a part, or all of our life, to change and we desperately want to get out of where we perceive ourselves to be now and get to somewhere new, it's much harder to see the 'trees for the wood'. Our focus can shift entirely to the bigger picture and not acknowledge the important smaller steps in between.

Plants don't grow instantly and neither do we. Change is a gradual process, that you have to allow, trusting although you can't see, that it's happening.

Allowing The Avalanche

I struggled with trusting the gradual process, just as much as my clients did, but I learnt to remind myself when I get into a fluster between the fear that nothing will change and the desire to keep going, change is like a snowball becoming an avalanche.

Small intended steps forward gradually build momentum to success, but if we rush and force the process we fail. We end up blocking the building energy and so it doesn't have the sustainability to last!

Instead, when we let go and allow the momentum to build with each new step towards our intention, like a snowball rolling down a mountain growing in size until it becomes an avalanche, it eventually increases so much that it sweeps us up with it and the energy carries us along towards our destination; no longer needing effort, just inspired action and trust!

Faking It Versus Building Lasting Experience

In my mid-twenties I entered the business world and dashed around with blind audacity. I sometimes succeeded on a surface level. I was a Company Director by 26 and an integral part of a very successful fast-growing internet start-up because I had a great 'can do' attitude, but inside I spent the whole time feeling like a fake, BS'ing and waiting for people to find out! I felt insecure because I knew I didn't really have the foundations and experience to sustain my new heights, so falling off my lofty perch was inevitable.

Compare this to my professional riding career which took 20 plus years to gradually build, starting aged four. By the time I was nine I was mucking out at the local riding school in exchange for free rides and lessons. I grew, trained and competed, as I moved up through the ranks of ponies, then horses, putting in the love, passion and time into something I naturally enjoyed, connected with and so felt committed to.

At 16 I groomed for my first international show jumper. Then at 17 I left home and started at the bottom of the professional level as a working pupil for an international rider and over the next 7 years I worked and trained my way through three different Olympic medallists and international riders to compete full time as an event rider.

Why The Rush?

When we get caught up with trying to make a sudden change, it's because we don't want to really feel the difficult emotions of growth. They're called growing pains for a reason because we are outgrowing our current situation, ready to grow into our new one!

When we first learn to walk we try wriggling on our bellies, bum shuffling, crawling, then standing up, staggering holding a hand, then staggering from one stable object to another to walking freely and then with confidence. Every gradual phase is important in our development, so that we learn the skill, get physically stronger, more balanced and create new neural paths in our brains, all of which translate to additional areas of our lives as we mature, We must fall down, bump into things and get a little bit hurt and frustrated, to drive us on and learn.

Without those uncomfortable feelings of the gradual, the desire to be free and walk, or walk further, explore, problem-solve, be independent and the frustration that we keep making mistakes and hurting ourselves a little, we'd never bother to keep getting up again and again and keep going and gradually improve.

All of my clients have found personal work uncomfortable and a struggle, they don't believe it will change, then suddenly without realizing it's different and they feel great. During the process, they've stopped hiding and being afraid of those uneasy feelings, accepted the truth, let go and allow themselves to trust the process and have hope in the outcome.

Change Happens

The process of change never stops, even if we may try to deny or delay it, just the context changes. Once we've physically developed, so the focus becomes psychological, emotional, sexual and mental development in different areas of our life, as we outgrow somethings and need more and it's finding the sweet spot of being able to trust and go with the process and be self-aware of what needs attention

In horse riding, like in any sport, there are always high days and lows days and no matter how good you are, given the right situation and you can still fall off and land on your face. It's how you pick yourself up, get back on the horse and learn from it which matters - there is always tomorrow and another chance to do it differently and that is part of the process.

We have growth phases, cycles and spurts, so it's essential then to practice patience with the process and when the frustration or bruising gets too much you're trying too hard and forcing it. Take a break, walk away, let go and have some time to rest or do something easy and pleasurable. Tomorrow is another day.

Remember to focus on what's great in your life today, what or who makes you happy, feels good and thankful. Then all of a sudden it will happen when you least expect it, because you've built up the momentum and the outcome is inevitable, so just make sure it's something you want!

Chapter 6:
Directions To Happiness

As I was casually driving along the narrow winding lane, enjoying my post-run muscles, I gazed absentmindedly at the lush green fields and trees rolling by it was the most beautiful autumn morning and I was feeling good!

BEEP…BEEP! "What are they doing getting up in my face?"

BEEEEEP ….BEEEEEEEP!!!

I looked again into my rear mirror trying to see what this person problem was…"What the F**k? I'm on the wrong side of the road!!!!!"

After three months driving around France and Italy, I'd pulled automatically out onto the right side of the road, but now I was back in the UK and we drive on the left! It was me, not them…

I laughed to myself and raised my hand in gratitude to the guy behind me, whilst feeling a little embarrassed by my mistake, but within a second or so the seriousness of the situation hit home; a car appeared speeding towards me around the next bend!

By getting what I had thought was in my face, the driver had not only changed my silly mistake from being possibly a much bigger one, but had diverted the course of my life!

Are You Blaming When You Should Be Accepting?

I hadn't liked this intrusion into my life and my first reaction was blame and irritation. Sometimes though it's necessary for the universe to shout at us, through other people, if we're not paying attention!

That sense of someone being in your business can really upset you and the Universe will keep sending situations and people to get in our face, our business and irritate us to make us take notice and above all be inspired to take ACTION!

The Universe/Love/Life wants to give you what you truly need to survive and thrive, but are you really willing to let it?

With every therapeutic client there comes a moment of resistance when they ask for the truth of what is causing the blocks in their life, but they're not ready to hear it; to receive and absorb the new information.

They don't really want to stay with the old way of life, but they are afraid of finding out what they thought was right -- isn't! Believing that difference or change is not just either a simple mistake, an adjustment to the journey, or a point of growth, but a sinful failure!

Once we're enlightened with new information about our actions and choices, which are the cause of the current problem in our life, we then have a choice to take our power and act upon the change, which has already happened in our awareness. The resistance to new information is a normal part of the growth process, but to ignore the truth and not act upon it is how we get stuck, so the Universe will then keep sending louder and louder signs, signals and messages, to get us to pay attention, as an act of love, because we all need helping hand.

Would You Rather Be Happy Or Right?

When it's time to change the experience/situation you're in begins to feel like trying to fit into clothing that's too small. You might manage it, and try to shrink yourself to fit, but it'll soon become very uncomfortable and begin to chaff and cause more than irritation, but soreness and hurts, infuriates and agitates us into action.

Whilst on my travels a few years ago I stayed in the lush forests of central France in an old cottage with only a handful of very friendly French locals and a quiet life. I was hiding, resting and recharging and it was everything I needed and I had felt so safe and relaxed there. Then the time came to either move or find out if I could stay longer.

I didn't want to leave, but I went to move on, without exploring all my options, out of habit. I wasn't used to staying, no matter how much I was enjoying somewhere. The forest village was already the longest I had stayed anywhere, having constantly moved for the past two months. So online I found a house and location that sounded great, a bit of bargain with good amenities, only a few hours east of where I was. I had been afraid I didn't have a plan of where to go, so I booked it even though I felt unsure.

As I was getting in my car and saying my goodbyes the owner mentioned; *"It's such a shame you're not staying for another week, the house is empty until next Saturday..."*

As I pulled away my heart sank!

Hours later I arrived at the new location, having been delayed by traffic to be greeted by a house and location which didn't match the advertising! Described to have beautiful views and sitting on the river bank with photos taken so that it looked like it was adjoined to the garden. What she forgot to mention was that the house sat in a built-up area on a busy main road, which you had to cross to get anywhere including to the river bank.

I was met by the owner with a brusque manner and backhanded digs about me arriving late and making her wait! *"Oh no"* my gut cried out. I'd already paid to stay a week!

She began to show me around the house with an endless list of rules and regulations which she expected me to remember, but hadn't bothered to write them down herself! I began to long for the freedom of the forest and inclusive warmth of the French villagers I'd left behind. My previous cottage was cosy with a little wear and tear that made it homely; I certainly didn't have to worry about my dog and I making a mess.

After having shown me around the immaculate rooms, she asked out of nowhere for a security deposit of 400 Euros. This was twice the amount of the rental, just brushing off her surprising demand with *"oh I forgot to tell you in advance!"* I started to feel blind-sided and very uneasy; I knew I had made a terrible mistake?

Don't Endure And Suffer - Take Action

Unfortunately, though I've been ingrained with a belief; *'I must make the best of a bad situation* (out of guilt and fear of mistakes). This attitude has caused me a lot of harm and misery in the past; however, it is still a powerful belief which I have to consciously challenge; if I am aware and I wasn't. So I became Pollyanna and brushed the nagging thought away.

Time passed and I found one or two things to think it'll be fine; I've got the pool and the river is still there, it's a big house, maybe I just don't like it being different?

As my feeling of discomfort began to ease I settled to make dinner, only to be startled by the high screeching of a cat. I rushed out of the kitchen to be greeted by the owner's cat; hackles up, teeth bared and spitting at my rather timid dog.

Only twenty minutes early I had been enjoying the pool and Faith was curiously nosing around in the garden. Now we couldn't get out, as the cat was barricading the French doors. Understandably the cat was feeling protective of her very new kittens, something else the owner had forgotten to mention, her only interest in how my dog would behave.

Two hours later when the owner returned, now 10pm I mentioned her cat's behaviour, only to be brushed off with *"your dog will get used it!"*

Just then Faith tentatively sniffed her way back outside, believing the cat had gone away; she was then suddenly chased, cornered and attacked. A loud scuffle ensued as she tried to get away. The howl which came from her was heart-wrenching. She dashed past us into the house, down the stairs and lay cowering by the front door.

If I hadn't quite got the message that this was wrong for us and if there was any doubt (and there was, amazingly) that to leave may be the wrong decision, the cat continued to hound me all night wailing outside the window.

The final straw to overcome my guilt for changing my mind and standing up for what I want and need was the 7am wake-up call by the church bells next door every 20 minutes (something else that had not been mentioned in the advert!).

As I drove away I was instantly happy and once again relaxed. Within three hours I was driving through the small winding forest roads back to my cosy cottage with the smell of pine and pure spring water to be welcomed by smiles, a little teasing and the invite to a BBQ that night with the promise of the best weather we'd had in ages.

Love GPS

Yes we want to be challenged to grow, but that doesn't have to be hard work and struggle, believing we are in the wrong or right or failing or succeeding for being good enough or not! We don't have to keep playing old patterns of guilt for following our hearts and doing what is uniquely right for us and makes us happy.

Everything living thing vibrates at different frequencies as the energy of the world flows through it. However what makes people unique is that we have the capacity to speed up and slow down our physical vibration, through our choices, beliefs and behaviour.

The more we hold on to fear, guilt, shame, pain etc, the more blocked our energy flow (through our mind, body and soul), the lower and more weighed down our energetic vibration (like a tyre becoming flat) and that's all we can see - the block and not the way forward.

As soon as we begin to let go, not only does love energy begin to find a way in, unblocking the emotional blocks of the past, like drain cleaner, so we fill up again (and our tyre begins to pump up) and raise our vibration, but we begin to see the Love GPS pointers for the next step on our right path (and wrong direction) and heart desires, no longer blinded and controlled by the blocks.

They start off gentle and subtle, sometimes as little irritations and if we learn to listen and pay attention we can acknowledge the information, let go of the cause, navigate smoothly through life.

If we ignore and doubt our instinctual awareness to them then they become nagging to show the block, often the past guilt, fear, grief we are holding now onto being manifested visually in our lives, to let it go.

When we resist and ignore these 'sensory and physical signs' and instead hold onto redundant historic beliefs, responses and perceptions, we create an internal blockage, like constipation!

However, we are continually receiving vast amounts of energy and information, and inevitably energetic pressure will build, as the two forces meet. Like waves increasing in size and power in the sea, the energetic force increases until it clear its path, so the waste emotional energy an be released and love can flow out of us.

These internal blocks are always reflected in our physical lives and sometimes with an accumulation of uncomfortable, annoying, irritating and stressful incidents and interactions. All of which are trying to get us to wake up to our internal 'emotional business' to be acknowledged and taken care of, by stimulating the correct emotional and behavioural response, instead of resistance and avoidance.

The less 'blocks' we have the higher our vibe and therefore the faster our vibration and so the quicker we can clear any bits of block debris that may arise. Love is like WD40, lubricating everything so the easier we can be directed forward and get on with fully enjoying and getting the most out of our lives, instead of getting stuck in the struggle of past beliefs and old wounds. It is the difference between driving a really old estate car and moving our way up into driving a new Ferrari, with high-performance oil and fuel.

When we practice being aware and accept the truth of the love behind the nudge, signpost or universal wake up call, we can laugh off any mistakes or embrace the growth opportunity and do a bit of tidying up of any mess caused and get on with living our life, back on track with what's right for us, feeling happy and peaceful!

We have free will though, so the choice is completely ours as to what we want to accept, which path to take and level of vibration we choose to live in.

Chapter 7:
11 Essentials To Becoming A Confident Happy Adult

I used to feel painfully out of place; too big, too loud, too messy, too clumsy, too quiet, like an 'Ugly Duckling'. I felt so lonely and desperate to fit in, but no matter how hard I tried, I just didn't seem good enough! I had no idea who I was, but guilty for being never quite right for what other people wanted me to be.

The Damage Of Rating Appearances Above Feelings

Growing up my parents were financially well off, I went to 'good' schools, we had a nice house, lived in a good area and I was seemingly a bright, healthy, active, bold child with lots of friends.

However, I grew up in an era when *'what would the neighbours think'* and attaining other people's approval though seemed to matter far more to my elders and society than getting to know me and how I felt. So I did as I was told and I followed the norm. I kept trying to attain more impossible goals of beauty, admiration, lovers, money and career success with the expectation that this would make me happy.

Although I looked like an adult, I felt nothing more than a lost little child and so after the initial distraction I was always left with the familiar, acute emptiness and fear within. Finally aged 26 I started to do something about it.

Repair What Was Missed

I figured if I could start again, right back at the beginning I could find out why I'd felt most of my life desperately unsafe, lonely, confused, not good enough, terrified of making mistakes and always super alert to everyone's reaction? Which led me to who I am now. Over the next 14 years I explored what I really needed and the essentials I'd missed out on.

I've fought with the world and my faith, cried a river, let go over and over again, fell down, got back up, learnt more, walked away, made mistakes, hid, then tried again and slowly as the darkness faded I began to emerge -- now a beautiful, strong, swan I am proud of.

I had to grow up the hard way but learnt what it takes to grow up into a confident, happy adult. Amazingly it only takes 10 essentials to raise a child into a secure adult, who can stand on their own two feet. Brave, trusting in themselves, and curious about the world and open to sharing, connecting and playing with other people.

If we miss out on any or don't get enough, we get stuck and anxious replaying out history and patterns over again trying to heal that developmental stage or element we've missed, without the skills to do it.

It's never too late though to become a confident adult, free to be who you are and do what you want! We have to be brave and reach out to learn the 'life skills' we've missed by finding substitute parents to teach us how to grow up! Once healed and let go of, nature will do its thing and put us back on the path to become who we were born to be - thrive and grow into our abundance. It's just like cutting away the dead wood, so new growth can come through!

Give yourself to permission to receive what you need and allow yourself to let go and grieve for what was missed. Then your mind/body will naturally and automatically do the rest and when you least expect it, you will suddenly realize you've also become a swan - a secure, confident adult in mind and body!

So here you are. How to re-parent your INNER CHILD and a guide to raising secure adults.

11 Essentials To Raising Confident, Happy Adults (no matter what age and it's never too late)

1) Parenting – Is Like Gardening

Children are like flowers, they need a sturdy flower pot, filled with soil full of goodness and water and exposure to space and sunlight. The role of the parents is to be the pot – sturdy and with enough room to grow [of course the size of the pot adjusts to the child's growth and eventually they must find their own pot]. The parental relationship is the equivalent of the soil to hold and nurture the seed, as it develops roots and begins to shoot upwards towards the light and grow in strength. So make sure to protect your child and we all need a home where we feel safe.

Tip: I highly recommend Stephen Biddulph's books to all adults, especially **The Complete Secrets To Happy Children**.

2) The Flower Pot – Parenting Starts With You

To feel safe a child needs to feel that their parents are secure in who they are. Secure means balanced; focused on yourself and taking care of your emotional and physical needs. Your child is dependent on you to survive, but you're supposed to be independent, self –sufficient and sustained by a well-rounded life and other people who are your equals. If your world revolves around other people and you dash around trying to please everyone, then you feel like the leaning Tower of Pisa - off balance and potentially unsafe to be around.

The pot must be upright, sturdy and relaxed – not anxious and stressed out, as this creates cracks in the pot, so take time for yourself and know what makes you happy and give yourself pleasure and kindness. Happy parents really do create happy children.

3) Soil Full Of Goodness - Accepting Your Mistakes and Theirs

Parenting can never be perfect and perfection should never be strived for, because just like anything in life you get better at it the more mistakes you make.

Mistakes are an essential part of learning, assessment and the outcome that you're trying and willing to learn. You not only want to encourage your children to try their best and make mistakes – remember a flower does not grow in a perfectly straight line, it makes adjustments as it grows in spurts – so accept that it's OK for you too.

- If you do these 10 things 60% of the time you will result in raising a secure adult.

- You can make a ton of mistakes (not dangerous of course) 40% of the time…

- As long as 20% of that time you repair the damage by admitting your mistakes, accepting that they are just errors, not punishable by death and persecution, and say sorry if needs be -- Including to yourself and your child!

Like in life, the most detrimental faults in parenting happen, when adults can't admit they've made a mistake, or don't know how to do something. We make a bigger mistake, simply because we don't ask for help. Stay stubborn and we can end up bottling up the guilt for not being perfect, which the child picks up on and in turn, learns that mistakes are bad, they must be perfect and if not they'll be punished for it! Forgive yourself and your child you're both learning as you go.

4) The Flower Pot – Setting Stable Boundaries

The boundaries of the pot are essential for the seed and soil to be contained, so know your boundaries! Children need good clear guidelines which are not just set out in words, but by actions. They mimic and mirror what they're demonstrated and what response other people get for their behaviour and what response they get. If it works and gets their needs met, even if the behaviour is negative and destructive they will keep doing it, so make sure to recognise and reward the behaviour you want and admire. Think long term, what kind of adult do you want raise? How would like them to behave towards themselves and other people?

Always keep it simple and have clear household rules in child-friendly language (Seven maximum, with an awareness of age) on unacceptable and acceptable behaviour, which will teach life skills on respect, taking responsibility and that there are consequences for our actions – positive and negative.

Such as;

- We do not hit other people
- We do not call other people mean names (swear, insult, etc.)

- It's OK to make a mess, but we tidy up afterwards etc.…

- We say sorry if we've made a mistake and hurt someone

- We are always honest - no exceptions…

- These boundaries must also include personal space boundaries – such as;

- "Knock and ask to come in, if a door is closed"

- No means No

- Yes, means YES

Write them up on a big sheet, board or have it made into a picture, so that it is clear and can be referred to by everyone in the family.

5) The Flower Pot – Consistency

Consistency is how firm the pot is. It's all very well if you have boundaries and rules and bedtimes etc, but if you don't have consistency if will all fail. Inconsistency is the killer of healthy parenting, because without consistency children feel confused and unsafe.

Parenting after protection and providing is predominately about teaching and nurturing - teaching your child to be a healthy, self-sufficient adult with the skills to survive and thrive in the world and nurturing their individuality.

Therefore, your job is to teach clearly, repetitively, appropriately to the age of the child and kindly.

- Always say what you mean clearly and mean it!

- No means no – don't backtrack, change your mind, and think before you use it! If it gets ignored, then back it up with short term consequences which a child their age understands.

- Yes also means yes, so openly encourage and praise their small daily steps into the world being more and more independent and brave – remember you're their coach and you want them to win in the game of life!

6) The Flower Pot – Give Permission To Be Real

Children are the best lie detectors you will ever find and they only learn to lie because you do. They're super sensitive to their environments, emotions and energetic vibe because they focus predominantly on their right brain. So when you hide or disown your feelings it confuses them, because they can feel something is wrong and naturally feel they have done something wrong and need to fix it.

So don't lie. Be honest and real - happy, sad, angry or scared. Take ownership and responsibility for your emotions by acknowledging, listening and expressing them appropriately. Bottle them up and they're out of your control and get projected onto others like a shadow only you can't see. Instead teach your child emotion intelligence, one of their essential life skills to surviving and thriving by demonstrating that it's OK to feel. Show them how to take responsibility by taking care of your own emotional needs.

Big Boys are allowed to cry and girls are allowed to get angry and we all get scared!

Your child won't be confused because how they feel being with you and how you feel to them matches what you are saying and how you are behaving. Just remember though your child is not there is to make you feel better, they're not your best friend, confident or shoulder to cry on; they're dependent on you not the other way around!

7) Soil Full Of Goodness - Fuel Your Child Right!

We all need a well-rounded diet. Everything we consume is fuel to burn off with body function, repair and growth, brainpower, and fitness to survive and thrive, otherwise it's just waste. Would you put the wrong fuel or no fuel in your car and expect it to keep running?

A child's digestive system is super sensitive, and so are many adults. So if you don't want hyper children, who can't concentrate, then don't give them too many stimulants! Stimulants include sugar (especially in sweets, cakes, biscuits, chocolate, but also natural sugars such as orange juice) caffeine and chemicals from processed, easy to grab foods and colouring. Keep it NATURAL majority of the time and encourage being active and they will stay balanced and healthy. It doesn't have to be perfect, but what you put in is the response your going to get.

8) Soil Full Of Goodness – The Power of Sleep And Rest

Without enough sleep, a child's brain or body cells do not repair, grow and function. A recent study showed that a child of 10 years who regularly has 10 or more hours sleep is more intelligent, alert, able to learn and process information than a child who goes to bed later and has less.

We all need plenty of sleep for our bodies and minds to function at peak form, but children need far more sleep than adults to keep up with the mental, emotional and physical growth. The same goes for adults who are unbalanced, insecure and stressed out!

Hours slept before midnight are worth twice as many as those after, so as well as making sure they have plenty of downtime through the day (unstimulated by electronics), get your child to bed nice and early. Set clear regular, consistent bedtimes, allowing for at least 40 mins self-soothing, quiet downtime, no TV, no computers, so they can unwind before sleep. It will not only help them learn better, but they can also cope better with the stresses and excitements of the day.

9) Soil Full Of Goodness - Permission And Acceptance

A healthy secure upbringing is based on giving the child permission to be themselves and explore their individuality. How they feel, think, create, play and work things out and express themselves without judgement and criticism, within a secure environment. Just like the shoot blossoming into the flower, allowed to explore its desire to grow, but securely supported by the flower pot and rooted by the soil.

Remember for your child their day, from the moment they wake up can end up being a barrage of being told what to do, where to go, how to do it, hurry up, don't rush with good and bad, right and wrong being banded around. This onslaught can end up giving them very little resilience or confidence to be able to work it things out for themselves, so they stay dependent and afraid.

Make sure to allow your child everyday time and space [appropriate to their age] to be free, explore, play and have some limited choices, so they can practice with their own power and independence and gain confidence.

10) Soil Full Of Goodness – Love In All Ways

Love is the core substance that weaves through all you do as a parent and in your family, but it also must be there for you, as an individual.

When we love ourselves and demonstrate that love in our actions and thoughts towards our selves we can not only love freely and abundantly those in our care without fear and control but also we teach children that it is important to express love to themselves too, just as they are, male or female!

It is this which creates security and confidence in knowing and trusting who they are as they grow up. It enables them to forgive themselves for making mistakes and being happy with wanting to grow, be bolder and braver in the world.

The child's desire and development process from early dependency into independence is simply *"pick me up, put me down, let me go"* which needs to be mirrored by the parent, but this can only happen if the adult is secure in themselves. It can be hard to let go, but that is the greatest act of love.

Love can be demonstrated in many forms, but the most important for a child to develop is the ones that make them feel safe, respected and encouraged. Never be afraid to express your love openly with anyone. Enjoy your children for being individual and never hold back on giving affection, praise, celebration, encouragement, reward, or from joining in with play and having fun with them. It is this which creates real love and bonding, instead of just need and dependency for survival.

11) Clearing The Dead Wood - Firm Love Is Also Essential

Never be afraid to balance soft love with the long term love of being firm (not tough, dominating, cruel or physical) and consistent, knowing that for your child's benefit it's better to have them hate you for minute or hour if you set a boundary or say no so that they can learn to love, respect and care for themselves later. Sometimes it seems easier to shout, criticise and smack, but all that instils is fear in your child towards you and the belief that disrespect and violence are OK. We can love unconditionally and correct certain behaviour that is either not safe or not respectful.

We all Need To Be Taught And Reflected

Ultimately I assume you want your child to grow into a strong, capable, considerate, respectful, courageous, healthy adult who loves, likes and respects themselves and others. Who will both embrace their own life and happiness and contribute to the world, which is the result of years of daily choices and repetitive teaching by you.

No one means to turn their child into a weak, cowardly, incapable, dependent adult, but it happens, because parents forget that children learn 80% of how to grow up by what they're demonstrated and how their parents respond to them. So don't parent by *"Do as I say, not as I do!"* and it will always be *"do as I do"* so instead do your best to show them how to live and love well!"

There comes a point though repairing the past and owning a new healthy future, where we need to be positively reflected and taught new information, just as a good parent would, so we need help.

We are grown up by others and the experiences with them, so if you feel you've got to that point because you've got stuck and "don't know" how to solve the problem, it is not a failure, because we all need at times to be taught new information or demonstrated a new skill by someone else first to learn, and then we can go off and practice.

Chapter 8:
How Trust Can Transform Your Life

Do you really trust, or are you secretly expecting the worst?

Trust is an act of choosing to be brave, letting go, and moving through fear and beyond to peace — to believe in the best outcome, without negative expectations based on the past.

Of course, there are always opportunities in life for harmful situations and to get hurt, but that doesn't mean you should spend it focusing on the fear of pain, waiting for it to happen or choosing to invite it into your life.

The Bright Side Of Life

Expecting the worst doesn't protect us from pain, instead it projects a looming wall of FEAR — of being hurt and disappointment until it's all we can see and all we receive.

Whereas looking on the bright side of life means you choose to focus your attention on joy, happiness, love, and trust in the beautiful way life always works out for the best when you let it! You get more of what you focus on, so are you willing to let go, give the benefit of the doubt and believe in the best in life, love, other people and above all yourself?

Seeing From Your Heart Not Your Eyes

Whilst on my travels last year I met a couple who were also travelling, both keen to experience new cultures, meet new people and explore. The difference between us was they were both blind.

Every step they took was literally an act of trust in the other, in life and the people around them. They didn't see themselves as disabled or lacking in any way, but simply that the world was worth exploring and they trusted that everything would work out. Their vision was clear, even though they could not physically see!

Walking Towards The Dark Side

Some people like to say that trusting is delusional and it is, if we ignore our natural instincts and physical responses which communicate to us what is safe or unsafe, harmful or loving.

At 19 I was offered an incredible apprenticeship. A live-in job located in the most beautiful surroundings and which seemed like a dream come true. I thought I'd landed on my feet, even when I met my soon to be boss who I thought she looked a bit hard and tough, I was swept away by the advertising. Then I shook her hand as I went to leave, it was limp, cold and my body literally recoiled.

It had been such a strong instinctual response, my other senses had already given me little niggling warnings which I brushed away, but this physical reaction was really hard to ignore. I was so afraid though that I would miss out and that there might not be another 'great opportunity', so I squished it down and accepted the role anyway.

Instead of growing in confidence and skill I spent the next 3 years in a painful environment of jealousy, bullying, lies and disappointment. My self-esteem hit the floor and I was having panic attacks for a year by the time she fired me, all of which I hid from my family because I believed it was my fault and I must have been in the wrong.

I repeated this pattern over and over again placing myself in destructive, unhealthy and unloving situations and relationships because I ignored my natural intuition and went with the image I was being sold.

Eventually, I accepted the truth that actually my gut was always right and the only thing I was doing wrong was ignoring it and going towards the thing it wanted me to stay away, instead of trust that something better always comes along.

When we actually listen and respect our gut instincts then we can simply let go, trust and act, by moving toward or away from situations without placing ourselves in harm's way.

Forgiveness Lets Trust Happen

To begin to trust myself, life and other people once more I had to forgive and let go of the guilt I felt for my mistakes and the idea that I was always in the wrong. I forgave my boss for her actions and other people who had been destructive because they simply mirrored my projection of attack and fear.

By forgiving I was not choosing to be weak, but instead I was taking my power back and choosing freedom. Without forgiveness, we end up simply meeting every opportunity and second chances for our growth, happiness and love with fear blinkers and a closed heart ready to turn away before we've even seen the opportunity in front of us.

Now as long as I listen and act on my physical and emotive responses and trust when it tells me someone/something is right or wrong for me, without doubt, or question I no longer have to be afraid of getting hurt.

Your World Is A Reflection Of You

When we hold on to the fear, guilt, pain and disappointment from our past we allow it to cloud our minds and hearts until we see a world around us that mirrors those fears. We project expectations of attack and rejection until we become blind and deaf to the love, beauty and amazing opportunities available to us.

We separate and isolate ourselves from other people in fear of being hurt, but still get exactly what we expect; struggle, judgement, failure, pain and loneliness, instead of what we need to be happy, healthy, and confident.

Choose to embrace a trusting, open state of mind and loving heart to yourself and you will not only attract but will choose boldly more of your own reflection from the world.

So do you like what you see …?

Changing Your Reflection

Are you ready to challenge your negative framework and choose to create a new one which is based on trust and receiving what you need?

You may have grown up in an untrusting or unsafe home, school or culture filled with other peoples fear, anger and a sense of lacking, but that doesn't mean you have to keep living your life from this experience. It was just someone else's perspective of life; it doesn't mean they're right and you're wrong for wanting joy, love and peace!

Putting it into practice

Whenever you feel fear, anxiety or negative voices creep into your mind and body – stop and take action.

- Place the palm of your left hand on your chest, so you connect with yourself

- Take a huge deep breath in — hold…

- Say out loud with conviction " I let go, trust and believe that everything will work out for the best for me"

- Then breathe out loudly and forcefully and let everything go -- repeat 2 or 3 times more until you feel more relaxed.

- Take small brave steps

Confident happy people are confident and happy, because they trust that they are liked and loved and the world is safe. They trust that they can cope and roll with life's plan, if things work out differently than they might have hoped, without losing trust that it will work out for the best for them in the end.

So stop letting fear win and trust. Reach out and reconnect to the people in your life who genuinely love and like you who you may have pushed away or moved away from; trust that they want you in their lives.

Go to work with a clear state of mind, no negative expectations and approach your colleagues with a friendly smile, trusting they're pleased to see you too and if your job feels like a wrong fit, then trust your instinct and look to change it!

Greet your lover, partner, spouse each day with trust that their doing their best and accept that if it unfortunately not enough for you then it's time to leave and trust you will both be OK. Be glad to see your children every day, let their enthusiasm for life inspire you and trust your instincts that you know how to help them be strong, secure, happy and healthy.

Radically transform your life, starting today, by knocking down your barriers which you have insanely believed protected you! Let go of the past, let go of the pain, let go of any past mistakes, forgive and open your mind to the beauty around you.

Embrace trust once more, so you can let go to a life full of love, joy, fun, opportunities and surprises — I guarantee it will radically improve your happiness from the moment you start taking action.

Chapter 9:
Why Patience Really Is A Virtue

I used to think patience sucked! I was taught growing up that it was a virtue, but I was never taught why.

In my experience, patience had meant I would miss out on something I desired. So I became the hare in the race and would fast track myself through career choices and opportunities and even relationships for fear that I would be forgotten and miss out again. Although in the story, it is the tortoise that wins the race, because he is constant and sure-footed.

With all my "hurry up" and haring around I may have seemed to the outside world to be go-getting and achieving great things that seem so valuable in our materialistic world. However I was so busy rushing to the next big thing, I was actually missing out on my life.

I was brought up in an era that has been all about getting it, having it, and then throwing it away. For a long time, this left me feeling empty. What I hadn't learned was the true meaning and purpose of patience.

Playing With Patience

So I took up the piano. After many years of wanting to play, and making endless excuses because I was scared of the hard work and the commitment it would involve, the time came when I was ready to face up to my fears. I told my piano teacher that if it took me until I was 70, that would be fine, as I believed it was a skill I would like later in life.

All good words; however, not how I behaved. As soon as I sat down on the stool and started to learn my first notes, I felt a building impatience. I would get so frustrated with my fingers and hands for not working independently. Every time I took a small step forward and improved, I would barely saviour the achievement and would once again get upset at anything I saw as failure.

My brain and body worked independently. For the first time, I came face to face with the realisation that I don't have full control over my body, and that it will only move at the pace it needs to go at. I was surprised by the dark feelings of self-punishment, criticism, fear, and anger. Through all this, my piano teacher demonstrated true patience to me, even if I had not gotten to grips with it yet.

For a year I went either weekly or fortnightly for this torture. When I felt enthusiastic I would practice between lessons, and if I didn't, well I would avoid it until just before the lesson or not do it at all. Of course, I would then be even more cross with myself that I couldn't do it.

Patient With The Challenge

As a former professional sportswoman, I knew that it took repetitive practice to get better at a skill. I used to think I was good with patience. The truth, though, was I was a natural rider with an affinity for horses and I had been riding since I was four years old, so I found it a pleasure to practice and, therefore, easy, but this was difficult, a new skill, and over and over again I wanted to quit!

Still, I wouldn't let myself. Even if I avoided practicing, I still kept turning up and paying the money. I had made a commitment to myself and I was determined to stick it out and see what would happen.

Through all this fight with myself, I came to discover patience. Patience is not a virtue; that makes it sound easy and light. No, patience is a challenge and it takes practice.

Patience is really about having the inner strength to stick to your guns when you know its right for you, face your fears, repeatedly let go of internal expectations, and have trust that it will all work out in the end.

Patience is not waiting, which is a dead zone, a place of inertness, hoping for something to happen to us. Patience is about committing to moving forward in small stages, no matter how slow you go, but to keep moving, even when you can't see the destination or outcome yet, but trusting that you will.

Slowly my hands and brain learned to adjust and they began to work in harmony - well, almost! I began to be able to read the music without looking at my hands and use both of them at the same time independently.

Even as I write this, I realize that I haven't truly acknowledged what a hard feat that actually is. It was like learning to walk again, but with my hands. Gradually, as everything started to come together just a little easier through patience and practice, I began to hear the music I was creating.

Patience With The Music Of Life

For perfects moments I would feel pure joy and pride; notes on a page, which could only become music because I learned to add space and timing. And like that, a door opened to a new understanding of life.

The music that is our lives can only be fully recognized, experienced, and played out when we allow space to move, breathe, and enjoy. We need to let go and let time play out at its own rhythm.

When we rush around, losing patience, we miss out on the enjoyment of the moment, as I had. We also miss our own individual melody and all the experiences, feelings, and people which help to create it. So I am now practising to be a tortoise, constantly moving, surefooted and enjoying a more natural pace—which allows me to look around and smell the roses if you don't mind me mixing metaphors!

After a year I could play Beethoven's 'Fleur De Lis', not perfectly, but well enough so that I enjoyed playing it and could hear in my soul what Beethoven was expressing when he wrote it. I still have my goal that I will be able to play well by the time I'm 70, but I am taking the time to make small steps in mastering the skill and enjoying the journey.

The practice of patience has dispelled my fears of inadequacy and by learning to harness and contain the energy of both fear and enthusiasm; not run or hide from it, but to own it and concentrate it into a powerful force, which consistently and steadily drives me forward in my life, towards my goals now measured at a pace which makes me feel both confident and appreciative of the journey. So perhaps patience is a virtue after all when we find our own route to truly understand it.

Chapter 10: Discovering Your Place In The World

The world is like a giant house party and we've all been invited and it's our job to find our right place and people to hang out with for our happiness.

Different Perspectives

Like all parties, there are some who turn up bringing a bottle, maybe food, and definitely with the attitude to add something to the experience. Then there are those who don't want to bring anything to share, but expect to be supplied with what they want or take whatever's going.

Some will want to hang out in the main room, get the party started, shake their stuff to some loud tunes, sing along, get hot and sweaty jumping around with joy. Whilst others will try to hang out in the corners just observing the party, unsure of participating, but may warm up and be braver with time.

Others love to hang out in the kitchen with all the food and booze and enjoy all the comings and goings, so they can connect and talk with the moving traffic of people. Whilst some will hang out in the garden huddled around a big fire, telling stories, singing songs and enjoying the warmth and the stars.

Or those who hang out outside in the garden in the dark, doing their best to look cool and aloof. Even though they do really want to be at the party and be with other people, they don't really want to look like they're having a good time, as though it's a weakness! They will attract others to share in the cigarettes, drugs or sardonic humour to justify having a guilty kind of suffering pleasure!

Then there are those who want to pretend that they weren't actually invited to the party and that they don't already belong. Seething with jealousy at those having a good time and getting along, so they get really drunk and aggressive and want to pick a fight with anyone and everyone!

At the bottom of the garden, filled with resentment and fantasizing about how to control or destroy the party, the house and everyone in it, you'll find those people who feel so scared and guilty for wanting to have fun and so blame everyone else!

Finding Your Place With Your People

We need both 'home' - the type of people and places which are restful and like snuggling into an old jumper and "the world" the types of people and places where we can explore, challenge and play.

So we need to test whom and which environments we are most at ease and comfortable to enjoy simply being ourselves, and those which stretch us to be more. In an intimate lasting relationship, we need a bit of both and the capacity for both people to change in needs and desires.

As we grow up we open and close our hearts to loving ourselves and valuing our own life. So sometimes we get fully involved in love and other times we make choices to avoid it, as we try on being different people and work out who we really are.

When I was younger I was a party starter. First on the dance floor etc. and flitting around as a butterfly, because I love meeting people, chatting, laughing, making others feel good by enjoying them! (this is how I travel too...)

For a while, though this behaviour shifted from loving life to the addiction of feeling high and being seen and I PARTIED a bit too much; hard — sex, drink, smoking and drugs! Then I began to feel bad/guilty. I felt guilty for going too far in my desire to love life and not loving myself. So I kept trying to fit in with the aloof group in the darkened garden working really hard at making them all happier and get their party started instead!

I totally dimmed myself down and so the people I attracted were a bit fake and felt cold, harsh and a bit mean, who mirrored my guilt. Any sexual relationships quickly became boring, unless a bit of drama was injected to make them more entertaining.

Then my life began to split, I would go travelling I give myself permission to be me and returned to loving life and so it was ok for me to hang out in my right places. Slowly I calmed down and gradually became more comfortable and relaxed in my skin and it took far too much energy to be anything less than real. So I became attracted to only be around people with whom I felt at ease -- open, honest, genuine people!

However, when I came home I would once again dim down and move towards men and women who matched my guilt patterns. Eventually, I became exhausted by all this behaviour and stepped out completely and stood on the side-lines observing.

Taking Time Out To Reassess

Taking time out allowed me to reassess my life and behaviour choices and forgive. Stepping back and slowing down allowed me to get more emotionally intimate with myself and know who I really was and trust my choices, so I found balance in my pleasure and enjoyment.

I can now move between the social butterfly, dancing queen, to hanging out the kitchen or sharing stories by the fire. I no longer have any attraction to standing on the side-lines or punishing myself with self-sacrificing.

When we finally accept our true nature, who we are at our core, what we enjoy short term and what will continue to make us feel good long term we can move towards not only the group but the kind of person which suits and reflects us - being ourselves intimately. To achieve this, we have to fully accept, forgive and let go of our choices of the past, if they didn't reflect LOVE for ourselves or others.

Once I accepted that it's OK to love me and be me everywhere in my life I began to attract people who not only enjoyed me being me and my love for life, but they were also happy with who they are and wanted to enjoy LIFE too.

It's essential to go both too far or not enough on our journey to find the balance of being our happiest and fullest versions of ourselves. It is only through discovery that we find both the peace and play of our unique place in the world and realise we have total control as to what we allow into our personal space and lives!

1) This is my experience, but who have you been hanging within your friendships, your work life and your intimate relationships - is this who you really are?

2) Is it who you need around you to be happy moving forward - do they mirror you being you as your true nature?

3) What choices have you not forgiven yourself who are holding you back from enjoying the party of your life?

Chapter 11:
Embracing Your Passion

As I pulled on the reins there was nothing.

I desperately needed to check my speed before we reached the jump; a bounce of two 4 ft. hanging logs into the water. I tried over and over again, as we flew down the hill, but to no effect!

This was my big day. The TV crew, spectators including my parents with the manager of The British Eventing Team, my boss, and sponsors all stood waiting at the water jump. I had dreamt of this since I was four. I spent years training, sacrificing everything and working my way up to be a professional event rider and this was my opportunity to prove myself to everyone!

I'd had been so focused on my excitement, the nerves of fulfilling everyone else's expectations and getting a fast time, that I had let my horse get away from me. She had been building momentum and now it was too late. I had lost control and we were no longer a team.

As she aimed herself at the approaching logs, energy pumping through her body, she bounced so high that she cleared them with feet to spare, but nose-dived into the water. Although she was fine, I had been nothing but a rag doll sent flying through the air until I landed face down in the water and drifting into unconsciousness.

What followed was a lot of drama, embarrassment and shame, but this wasn't the last time I made this mistake.

A Rose By Any Other Name

We like to call it passion, excitement, drive, focus, competition, maybe it sounds more romantic or less daunting, but it's all DESIRE!

Desire gets a bad rap, but it's a wonderful emotion. It's our life force, our lust for life, joie de vivre and makes us find reasons to get up in the morning!

Desire is our ability both to create (grow) and destroy (consume). It is neither bad nor good, but we do need to learn how to master it. The greater the desire we feel, the more force it has, the more we need the courage and skills to harness and direct it.

But like a learner being given a Ferrari to drive, I lacked the experience and skills to be in charge, so I ended up out of control and crashing!

I was to repeat this again was when I was totally bowled over by my feelings of love and complete sexual attraction for a man who came into my life. I got completely carried away by my excitement, passion and fear of failure that instead of having a little patience to let it build and grow naturally I tried to rush the pace of the relationship between us and ended up with what I most feared; broken-hearted!

Desire is essential to survival and the ability to thrive and be happy in life. Take hunger our most basic desire, the desire to consume. We must fulfil it to live and grow. Hunger tells us when we are not getting enough of what we need and we must listen. Hunger is not only for the right food (thirst is the also hunger) but also affection, recognition, attention, play, rest and sleep.

Sadly, we can fall into the trap of giving too much and not receiving enough. Giving all our energy and time away, whilst blocking ourselves from being fed, so we end up starving and anxious.

However rest assured the Desire force will kick in to fight back, survive and rebalance. Enabling us to create personnel boundaries between ourselves and other people. It gives us the power to say no or demonstrate NO in action, so we are in charge of our lives and we don't become smothered by other people.

Desire's force to destroy used correctly enables us to clear, cut away, and let go. To not hold onto things, experiences, emotions and choices that we have outgrown, no longer need and is dead or dying. Both these sides of the force of Desire empower us to create space to invite new possibilities and ideas into our lives and initiate change.

Riding The Creative Force

We are all creative beings whether that's to create relationships, a baby, building a career, a business, a home, a piece of art, a book, making love and creating an orgasm! It is in our nature to express and fulfil our unique desires for life, but if we lose total control of ourselves we ultimately get burned by a fire that's raging!

To become empowered is to know how to manage the pace and force of our desires enough to have momentum, movement and flow in our lives, without getting carried away too much to lose control of the direction and purpose and that only comes from trial and error.

However, if we are afraid our desires and we repress, hide or avoid them we leave its force untamed and out of control. We end up redirecting our energy into our FEARS instead. Either trying to grasp, manipulate, dominate, or control other people or situations to force an outcome, or instead, turning it on ourselves to self-sabotage and destroy our own lives.

If we try to squish our desire out shame and guilt, the result is stagnation, depression and starvation, like a river being damned, unable to flow.

By embracing our desires and learning to not be afraid of the fire behind them, but instead respecting it we can learn how to play with it we can master how to harness the powerful energy for our benefit.

We can become a team with our desire able to still keep the momentum, but with enough control to communicate thought, skill and judgement like my horse and I needed to be. I could then have not only successfully completed that water jump but most importantly the rest of the cross country course and achieved my dream.

Chapter 12:
The Masculine & Feminine Blueprint

One of the biggest blocks to SELF LOVE, self worth and loving another is how we feel about our own gender and our opposite and the differences between the masculine and feminine that reside in us both.

We can have certain expectations and beliefs that we've built up over our lifetime regarding our own gender and the opposite gender based on our relationships with our parents, grand parents, caregivers, and siblings.

The relationships we then attract and seek are founded on that belief pattern positively and negatively regarding the male or the female gender; expectations of how you expect them to behave towards you, themselves, others of the same sex and how they interact together.

Gender Identity

Over our lifetime we've created in our unconscious mind a subtle, yet very powerful and highly emotionally charged blueprint which influences how we see part of ourselves, our own bodes and the partners we choose, until we become more conscious about it.

Its like this if your are a woman and in early childhood or adolescence and you observed and experienced your mother, grandmother or other women show passive aggressive sexual jealousy, bitchiness, cruelty, abuse, cold, disconnection from their own sexuality, self loathing or rejection of femininity, subservience you're going to have on some level taken in those negative, lacking beliefs around women. And will embody that in your own mind, body energetically & emotionally.

We take theses message in both with acceptance and resistance to being like them to create this blueprint about your own gender and that will have a very negative, impact on how you yourself or other women, as friends, bosses or lovers.

Of course the same is true is what you observed and experienced was the opposite; nurturing, kind, empowered, confident, brave, loving, open, proud of themselves and embracing of their sensuality and sexuality, wild and spiritual, focused, and had equal partnerships.

The same is also true for the opposite gender. Say as a woman and I saw my dad /grandfather/brothers/other care givers or important role models being, cold , distant, unavailable, very busy, absent, domineering, controlling, saw women as less, was, aggressive, alcoholic, violent or abusive. It would create a very negative perception of the masculine and I'm going to embody which will make it very difficult to trust a man in any form of relationship, especially if I am wanting to date and be intimate with one.

With a blueprint like this you will keep attracting based on a deep sense of distrust and emotional wounding. They may not behave in exactly the same way, but there's going to be the sense of disappointment, their sense of being let down, or being unsafeness.

If the picture of the masculine is one of being secure, trustworthy, bold, fun, playful, brave, confident, stable, reliable, emotional, loving, nurturing, kind, empowered, demonstrate equality with women, self love for being male etc. All those positive qualities will create the blueprint for the gender.

A Mixed Bag Blueprint

The truth is most of us have a mixed bag of experiences which build up this blueprint, some of it helpful and some it hindering. Some of it drives us forward to be different and more, or holds us back. Some of it gives us strong trustworthy foundations about who we are and who to trust and others leave us with gapping wounds in our identity.

For example, if you had a mother who you thought was incredibly loving and caring, but you also recognise that she put herself last and over-gave and lived a life completely in service to everybody else, to the detriment of herself. As a women will may have a negative belief that it's not okay to be powerful, to be confident, to be strong, to be in an equal partnership and you will absolutely find it difficult to trust in relationships because your disconnecting from your own worth and value as an equal.

Another example could be, if your father had been an incredibly balanced, grounded, open, loving man at home, but again he work too much and wasn't available you could have got a negative perception that men are all of these wonderful things, but also they're unavailable to you.

The Masculine & Feminine In Us Both

Now these blueprints also translated on to our relationship with the masculine and feminine energies inside of us and how we perceive the masculine/feminine of the Universe.

Its like this imagine a strong river flowing…

The masculine energy is the river banks, it is grounded, stable, offers clear boundaries and holds the river and it gives direction. The water flowing is the feminine energy. It can be smooth gentle, or fast and wild.

Within us the that feminine energy is the inner creative, spiritual, emotional and sexual energy. It is inner connection to your GPS and LOVE connection and flow. It is the intimacy of life.

The masculine energy is the physical realm manifested. The action, the form of things we create and desire, physical touch and expression.

So a harmonious unity between those feminine and the masculine within us is essential, just like the river banks and river.

If we are holding onto past painful woundings and negative blueprints on the masculine and feminine in our bodies and mind the harmony becomes imbalanced and just like the river it can dry up or the river banks can crumble.

We will be left feeling very unstable, insecure, anxious and unworthy of LOVE and incapable of attracting the partnership we desire or trusting that relationship, because we know are missing something.

As you move through this book and reconnect to loving yourself look towards reclaiming and loving the feminine and masculine parts of yourself, because what we feel within we always see reflected in our life.

Assessing Your Blueprint

This is really important so take some time now, be honest with yourself and write down all the ways you see and feel about MEN and WOMEN.

Think of your mother and father, grandparents, siblings and past lovers, close friendships and their behaviour, action and your experiences with them and you will begin to see patterns. Also see if this also connects with storylines in films or books etc that you like or thoughts and feeling you have about any celebrities, government figures etc.

These patterns are what have made up your blueprint, some of which is still active and driving your life choices and self perception in positive or negative ways, and others are dormant and might be worth reigniting or leaving well alone.

You will be able to tell by your emotional reaction and if you are still acting towards that the same way.

If you get angry it is because you have conflicting belief underneath what you're saying - so ask yourself WHY do I feel that way and ask again until you release the energy and reach a place of emotional neutrality and feel clarity. The conflict is usually between the LOVE within you and you experiences.

If you feel sad, this is because there is an unresolved emotional wounding in your body - just let the tears flow freely until again you reach calm and the on carry on.

Men - Positive traits/ experiences/beliefs	Men - Negative traits/ experiences/beliefs
Women - Positive traits/experiences/ beliefs	Women: Positive traits/ experiences/beliefs

This is a very personal self exploration and only you can be the guide of what is if right for you. It is a great way to trust in your own LOVE GPS which will always show to what resonate with your heart etc and who you really are at your core and how you want to show up in the world and attract back from it.

Don't hold back, be brave and take time over a week ideally as new thoughts and feelings bubble up as you begin to unlock your blueprint. It will lead you to forgotten treasures about yourself you can reclaim and be empowered by and release old wounds and thoughts that are no longer serving you .

You've got this and let LOVE be your guide, for it will lead to transforming your life.

Chapter 13:
10 Priceless Life Lessons

In this chapter I want to share with you my ten priceless life lessons; the kind that has changed my character not only in how I love myself, but how I choose to show up in the world. To be honest, I wish I'd learned them sooner.

1. Being Happy Is Not About Achievement

I had to start with this one, as someone who has spent so much of her life achieving, striving to achieve, and competing to win. The first half of my life I strived to ride for my country and compete in the Olympics, then to achieve in business, then academically, and always in relationships. It doesn't matter what I achieved. No job, promotion, money, relationship, house, highest mountain, or gold medal would ever change how I felt about myself.

Achievement is the icing on the cake, so it's important to learn to like the cake that's the sum of who we are first, so we have something to ice.

2. We Are All Doing Our Best

I used to hold myself to the highest scrutiny criticism and moral compass. I was excellent at delivering self-punishment as judge, jury, and executioner for every small flaw, mistake, or underachievement. However, I would forgive other people for every fallibility, choice, and indiscretion. I expected so little accountability or responsibility from other people and so much from myself.

I've learned to balance it out by being more lenient, forgiving, and loving toward myself and accepting that we are all doing our best—and this rule applies to me too.

3. We Have To Know And Respect Our Deal Breakers.

Self-worth is Love in action, so I got clear about my relationship deal breakers. Sadly, I've let a lot of people throughout my life treat me with disrespect—lie, cheat, take liberties, bully, blame, shame, and even abuse. I didn't stand for anything. I couldn't say no. Without no, my yes had no value. Now my deal breakers are respect, honesty, and responsibility.

When we know our deal breakers, we don't accept mistreatment because we know we're worth more.

4. Other People's Actions Aren't About Us

When I was in my twenties, my ex-fiancé cheated on me. For a long time, I believed it was my fault, that it must have been something I did or didn't do—that I wasn't good enough. I realize now that how any other adult chooses to behave is about them, not me. Yes, we were young, but my ex felt there was a problem in the relationship, and in response, he chose to be the kind of person who lies and cheats.

We're only responsible for our own actions, feelings, and words, which means the buck stops here, but this also frees us from wasting energy and time on cleaning up other people's messes.

5. We Need To Trust Our Intuition.

I've made many mistakes in my life because I didn't trust my intuition, nature's gift of survival, which helps us thrive. I got involved with the wrong people, relationships, and jobs, ignoring that I knew they weren't right for me from the start, and then paid the price by wasting time and energy trying to make them work.

Intuition can be as loud as someone shouting in your ear, and other times, it's more subtle. When we slow down, take our time, allow it to get clearer, and listen, we save ourselves a whole lot of trouble.

6. All The Studying In The World Will Never Be Enough.

I've spent years studying, seeking to understand people and the meaning of life, love, and the universe. I have letters after my name to prove it, and much of it was a waste of time. Most things are just stepping-stones to somewhere else, often on a cyclical path back to what you knew already. Knowledge is power, but experience in using it, applying it, seeing how it feels, and making mistakes trumps everything because that's wisdom.

Good old-fashioned hands-on living and having the courage to get involved and experience makes you wise. Then you have a beautiful lesson to share.

7. Face The Scary Stuff.

I wasted so much time hiding from the bogie monster, the scary truth inside of me. I just had to be brave and come face to face with how I felt and what I desired. I had to feel all that I had hidden, repressed, and buried instead of trying to unlock it all through my head with knowledge, or getting someone else to tell me what to do. Only then was I free; I could I stop caring if other people approved of me or not and just love myself and know what matters to me.

Life is at its core is something we do alone and by becoming our own best friend we no longer have to fear being unloved, because we are love, which enables to love and share our life with many people.

8. Accept That Life And People Are Inconsistent.

When I was little, like everyone, I was reliant on others and needed them to be consistent so I could feel safe in the world. Unfortunately, they weren't, so I got stuck needing to please other people so they would take care of me, but I always felt let down and disappointed. I was like a drowning young woman at sea, battered around by the force of the waves with nothing to hold onto, because I had nothing of substance to rely on until I learnt to be consistent and love myself.

Change is the only consistent thing there is. Accepting this empowers us to learn to depend on ourselves.

9. We Can Be Our Own Best Friends

By facing the scary stuff, getting clear about my deal breakers, starting to trust my intuition, and forgiving myself, I began to like, love, and respect myself. I turned my curiosity toward finding out about myself and what I actually like, enjoy, and don't want. I became my own best friend and I've got my back if there's a problem.

I came to know me, inside and out, and what matters to me, so I built a boat of substance and I'm no longer drowning. The world around me can be wild and changeable like the sea, but now I can ride out the waves without fear. The same can be true for you.

10. We Are Enough

I never needed to strive to be anyone's best friend, girlfriend, or wife by keeping a tidy house, cooking like a chef, and making wild passionate love every night, or by being a CEO, earning a fortune, or having a gold medal or a PhD. It sounds exhausting just writing it, but that was how I used to live my life.

Yes, I sometimes do some cool, fun, interesting stuff; I am curious about the world and enjoying my life. But sometimes I can't be bothered. I like to slob around in my PJs watching old movies. I get morning breath and matted hair but can scrub up well and attend the ballet. I now know who I am, what makes me happy, and the value I can bring to any relationship or situation, not because of what I do, but who I am.

We're unique, priceless and irreplaceable, and the sum of every experience. Our greatest relationship is with ourselves because it's through that relationship that we learn how to truly love other people, including our children. And when we demonstrate how to love us, we can get the most joy out of our lives.

Chapter 14:
Letter To Your 13-Year-Old Self

I would like to encourage you to take stock on all that you have read and learnt in this section. As you have discovered so much of our perceptions and the choices we make today come from conditioning and experiences in the past, and a crucial time for our self-development, sexual maturity and empowered is our teenage years.

This is the time when we leave being little dependent children and begin to spread out wings in the world. It is a phase in our lives when we explore ourselves, love and relationships, using what we have learnt at home and if it works and doesn't work in the wider world. It can be messy, complicated, fun, scary and full of possibilities, but if we've not had the support or guidance we needed at this crucial time we can become lost and confused.

We cannot change the past and protect ourselves from the choices we've made, but we can forgive, guide and love ourselves anyway. So I ask you to reflect and offer the loving parental or friend guidance to your younger thirteen-year-old self (of course it can be any teenage year that really matters to you)

My Partial Example:

Dear Jo-jo,

I want you to know that even though the years ahead may be hard at times and you may have to face some very grown-up, difficult experiences and painful losses, which will make you sad and lonely, you are so strong and capable and never alone.

I cannot change what you will go through, but there are no mistakes, so just trust that in time it will pass and the sun will shine so bright.

You are truly beautiful inside and out and never, ever think you are fat or too big. Do your best never to sell yourself short in any way. Yes you are different and different is wonderful and it's the differences that give you something to offer.

Follow your passions, your heart, your pleasure and do your best to take care of yourself and your body. Sex and intimacy will seem both scary and exciting and although you will make choices that don't always honour the love within you and you will kiss a few frogs. I know that in time you will come to realise who is worth offering your mind, body and soul to and why....

PART 2:
DATING WITH LOVE

Part Two Introduction: Dating With Love

Dating is the transition between loving yourself and allowing yourself to love others. It offers the opportunity to discover yourself on a deeper level, get clear about what's important to you and what you want to attract. It is the exploration to check out our skills to maintain a sense of balance, self-love and our new understanding of how love works, and what it needs from us. To practice our capacity to stay being fully ourselves in the presence of getting to know someone else.

In this section we will explore the essentials of 'I Matter and You Matter' - we are equals, but how much do we have in common and how much is different and what do I need to be happy?

We will look at the phases of love and relationships and the difference between dating based on power and achieving success in dating with love. Making choices and connections that we can feel really good about, as we allow someone to come closer and get more emotionally and physically intimate.

We can learn to date with love, whether we have been away from dating for a long time, or if we are already dating, or currently in a longer-term relationship which needs to refocus to love.

When we take the balanced steps to attract and move towards healthy loving connections in all areas of lives, as well as in dating, it is like opening the door and loudly expressing we are willing and ready to let love show up in our lives from other people and for love to flow through us.

Love will then show us through the Love GPS you've been learning about if we need to make some adjustments in our thoughts and behaviour, let go of some old wounds which are blocking our way and will show us the next step forward, preparing us to meet what is seeking us - the right person for our love connection.

NB: You will find at the end of the section a questionnaire designed to get you to really reflect on who you are and what truly matters to you when it comes to your life, dating and in relationships. I would suggest taking a look at this before you start this section and then review it once you've completed it and perhaps revisiting it once you've got out there and put somethings into practice. It is a good tool for ongoing review.

Chapter 15:
Why Loving Is A Choice But Love Isn't

LOVE is the uncontrollable force. It is the force of life, it is growth and connection and the essence of pure abundance. Even as powerful as we have the potential to be, and as important as we often like to believe we are, there are two things we'll never have control over; LOVE and DEATH.

The simplicity and magnitude are too enormous to truly comprehend, like gazing at the night sky. All we can do is be in awe and respect their force and purpose, and concentrate on what we do have a choice over - to be loving or not.

Loving Is A Choice

Loving is an act of kindness; consideration, care and respect! It is the choice of currency we choose to interact with each other and ourselves. It is the choice to open up and share our gifts of joy, laughter, honesty and individuality and a willingness to accept Loving from the people/animals and the world around us.

Loving is who we're naturally born to be as children, though Loving as an adult sometimes means making the tough choice to set a boundary or end a relationship, because LOVE is leading you somewhere new.

Love Just Is

Loving creates more loving, something we must have to be healthy, yet no amount of Loving though will create LOVE! Nor will any amount pleasing, entertaining, sex, planning, thinking, manipulation or bullying will make someone love you or you love them, because LOVE is not in our power.

LOVE happens to us! It might seem unfair at times, but LOVE does not forget, judge, hate, or punish. LOVE just is! LOVE has a plan of its own and resistance is futile. For LOVE time and the distance does not diminish its force, but increases it; like the swell building momentum, which is a clear sign it is love and not a phase of desire.

Even if we waste our energy to resist it, block it, halt it, delay it, deny it, turn our back on it, stop being Loving and close down because we're afraid of its power or that death will take love from us; at some point we all usually do, I've certainly tried - be assured LOVE will always win out!

Like sandbags trying to block an oncoming tsunami, our actions are nothing against its power. LOVE just like the water in a stream will wash over all manner of debris to clear its path, to become the river and then the sea.

Tenderizing you in the process to be ready for its planned destination.

So when your time comes and it will and LOVE chooses you, it's best to be brave and surrender; like the surfer riding the wave, just trust and do your best to stay as balanced as possible and let the wave carry you forward. Give it time to unfold; for the ocean always meets the shore, just as LOVE always finds its way.

Chapter 16:
Why Do You Want A Relationship ?

We can get so wrapped up when dating, wanting a relationship, and being in love that we can forget to ask ourselves WHY do we want it and WHAT for?

There is so much advice out there to vision what you want and how it will feel when you actually get what you want, that when it doesn't happen and you're not being asked out and being met by another, we can get really frustrated that the universe is not on your side. That you must be doing something wrong and unworthy of LOVE, but the simple answer maybe is that you are not ready YET!

But I'm ready I hear you shout, I'm sure of it, I know what I want, I've done the work!

But have you thought what you'd actually be able to offer to the relationship and someone else at this time?

- What is going on in your life?
- Are you getting your work/career to the next satisfying level?
- Are you going through some health issues?

- Do you have very young children that need your focus and care?

- Are your life and emotional state the kind of space you would like to invite another in and WHY?

Ask yourself WHY do I really want this?

It's in this honesty with ourselves that we can discover that want we really want is for them to either to ease an old wound we are carrying or play out on the old unhealthy pattern.

For example; "If I was in a relationship it would lighten my load and be supported." (Am I needing him to support/provide for me, because things seem difficult at the moment and I want it to be easier) — TRUTH: then in truth I am wanting a FATHER figure and so I can be a child and be take care of)

So it means there is some reflection, refocusing and self love to do because whatever is going on in your life it is actually an opportunity for your personal healing/growth to come into more of your true inner power, strength and above all balance as an individual, so you can be reconnected to the abundant SOURCE of LOVE and so in right timing be a healthy partner in an adult relationship.

LOVE needs you to own your voice, say what you need, be capable in your life and ask for help when needed. To be empowered and stand in your I MATTER so the YOU MATTER can exist and a relationship can be built.

The UNIVERSAL fact is if we were truly ready LOVE would align and flow and the relationship would unfold - Its that simple!

Being Stuck No Matter What

This can feel intensively frustrating and heartbreaking if we are stuck in pattern trying to get fixed and good enough for a relationship, which seems forever out of reach, feeling like no matter what we do it doesn't seem to change the situation…

But the key is in that statement - NO MATTER WHAT I DO - the blocked pattern of belief is that there is no matter, no I MATTER, so there is no connection to the flow and receiving LOVE. Literally, there is not enough YOU to ground LOVE into and flow through. No conduit for LOVE as the universal electrical circuit.

I personally know this pattern and it's the worst!

Working so hard to be loveable for a man to love me. That if I could sort my internal mess quick enough I would not miss out, or that I would be sorted and perfect and ready!

Ready at this time in my life meant being fixed! I wanted a relationship with a man so he would heal my old wounding around LOVE and bring Joy and fun into my life.

Unconsciously I still believed the HE/ Relationship to be the SOURCE of my real happiness and feeling good, instead of my relationship and connection to LOVE.

So those men I did manage to attract in at this time did not stick and they were not the kind of man I could have a lasting healthy relationship. They were just matching the needy vibe I was putting out. We were already not on an equal footing, because I was not really open to LOVE.

My head and inner being knew what a healthy loving relationship would be like for me - but I was living and behaving from an unconscious driving pattern that the complete opposite and coming to a false belief of lack of self-worth and lack of self.

Acceptance Of Where You Are At!

When I was ready to be honest with myself about the WHY, I saw that my thoughts, beliefs, desires and behaviours were not matching I could accept that the UNIVERSE and LOVE were right. I was not ready for a relationship! Not because I was not good enough or worthy, but because I was not completely in alignment with LOVE within me.

The shift happened the moment I made the decision that the right thing for me - what I needed and wanted was to be single for now and focus on loving my own self. That it was OK to be single! It was not a failure, but a success to choose me and give myself my complete attention, care and focus.

The universe had been making it clear, by blocking my efforts to have a lover and that my whole focus needed to be on the I MATTER phase and be my own lover.

Putting down the idea of being sorted enough to be loved by someone else, but instead turning all focus on me and accepting that my life needed me to all about me to heal, to be immersed in love for myself, to be sorted FOR ME instead. That I could be LOVED now!

I could finally accept then that I did not actually have the energy at this moment to be in a relationship, because I needed it all for myself. That being single was not only a good thing for me now but the right thing!

That it would not be fair to draw someone into a relationship with me at this time as I did not have the goods to offer to the relationship.

Putting down the striving meant I could stop wasting energy and accept that the UNIVERSE/GOD/LOVE knew better and I could lean back and trust.

Now perhaps you are ready to be in the ebb and flow of dating with LOVE and so it's OK to accept that the

LOVER connection will come in and out of your life for a while and so it's important to let it flow with ease by reconnecting to you LOVE in self.

Or maybe you are already in an established relationship, but communication is difficult and you seem disconnected then LOVE is showing you the same thing - come back to your I MATTER and love within.

Just being honest and accepting where you are at now takes the pressure off and lets Love do its thing.

When We Shift Focus Back To Love

For me, this small, but epic shift in perspective and acceptance LOVE energy began to quickly flow and I could see clearly that things would change when I was ready. Not because I was fixed and perfect, but because I was tending to my own needs first and so I would be an equal and open partner to another.

Once I shifted my focus back to the source of LOVE and the balance I needed, my resources of energy and capacity to deal with life and flow with ease and confidence bubbled up. I had shifted out of an old restrictive negative pattern of control and fear and back into the abundance of real LOVE.

I had been looking for love in the wrong place - seeing LOVE in the relationship, instead of having love, being the flow of love and then seeing the relationship follow suit naturally.

Of course, as you will have already come to understand from this book and your own experiences that as soon as we relax back into LOVE in ourselves, this is when the Universe starts to flow to you your desires.

So ask yourself why do you want that relationship? What do you believe it will bring you? Is there a deeper truth underneath that the Universe is trying to tell you?

Are you exactly as you need to be ready or are you are getting ready to be ready by focusing on you and your connection to LOVE?

Chapter 17:
Are You Ready For Love Again

As I stood on the edge of the sand looking at the waves, I felt the desire to get in, but wondered whether I'm ready?

I've been surfing for 13 years, but over the past few years, it's become sporadic. My interest waned because I became tired of the cold and fighting my way out back for what often seemed like little reward. Now though I am fitter, healthier, happier and more balanced in my life and gradually my desire has been building since I moved to overlook my favourite beach.

Just like my love for surfing, being open to love again after healing a broken heart, or just because we've taken some time out to focus on ourselves, can be daunting; no matter how much we desire the intimacy and connection once more.

My first step was to buy a new warmer wetsuit, so I could stop some of my excuses - the right equipment is essential!

The waves had looked good for the past few days, but I didn't have the time to get in and this built up frustration, which is a good sign. Now the sun was shining and the ocean was inviting and there was nothing in my way, however, I still felt apprehension.

When we begin to want to 'get back out there' we can often be fooled, believing we're still afraid of getting hurt, or that we're 'not good enough', when in fact what we feel is the nervous energy of excitement, desire and anticipation.

Even if we have still got some lingering and pointless anxieties, really what's holding us back from leaping in and giving it another go is our unsureness that we have the skills and knowledge to do it differently!

No one wants to repeat the same behaviour that caused what we may perceive as a failure; so we question:

- Can I maintain being myself?
- Can I be vulnerable and show who I really am and be OK?
- Can I stay balanced and not get lost in someone else, in their needs and happiness?
- Can I stand up for myself or ask for I need?
- Can I allow someone else to be who they really are, make mistakes and be imperfect and still love them?
- Can I fully forgive myself for past mistakes

Real Reservations

Of course we never really know if we're ready until we give it a try and test the waters. It's nice to watch the waves from the beach, but it's much more fun to be in the sea, splashing around!

A) If we haven't gone away though and reflected on how we approached and behaved in the last relationship, or all our relationships — what worked, what didn't and what do I need to change, then we can't expect to learn and do it differently.

B) If we haven't checked to see if we need to learn new skills and if so, go out and get some new instruction, information and guidance; then we can be sure that we will make the same mistakes.

C) If we haven't been practising with our new information and skills, by gently flirting, communicating, interacting, socializing etc on a regular basis in a relaxed manner to warm up then we can be sure that no amount of theory will mean we have the capacity to put it into practice.

We learn our love and relationship techniques growing up, but it's essential we keep reviewing our techniques as we get older and more experienced. It's a bit like driving, we can become complacent, lazy, pick up a few bad habits, forget things, or discover we've even completely missed out on some essential skills in our original training.

If we have done these things, then it's time to paddle out a little deeper, because no one can catch a wave from the shoreline and we need to let Love know we are ready for it to find us.

Working The Love Muscles

I know how to surf, even though I've not been on the waves for 9 months, but my body needs a chance to remember and feel the energy of the water, the board under my belly and the resistance of my wetsuit. My muscles need to be used and stretched and reminded of the action that only surfing needs; no amount of other exercise can make me really surf fit and the same goes with dating and love.

I don't expect to paddle straight out back and be able to grab the huge first wave that comes and be awesome! I don't beat myself up for not being the girl who used to ride 6ft waves, because then I used to ride almost every day, I was competitive and riding bigger rocked my world! I'm older and have different needs now.

What I can expect is to feel frustrated, excited, wiped out a few times, feel a bit breathless and exhilarated and when I get out of the water to be so relaxed and hungrier than I have for a long time. And I will definitely want more of it! This is what I got and today I went in again and it was a little better.

Think of yourself as a MUSCLE - to get the most out of you, you need to be given activity, pushed a little out your comfort zone, little and often until you become stronger, fitter and more filled with power and confidence.

We can always start small and just in the case of surfing choose a calmer day, wait for the tide to not be on the push [in or out], or stay on the edge of our comfort range and not go too far out back. This will feel safer, but there won't be many waves to ride, which will soon become boring. Yesterday the surf was a bit bigger than it had been the days before and it was the challenge and opportunity for me to test my skills, and it was that which brought up my apprehension!

We can keep waiting for the easiest person to date or choose what we think is a safe relationship, but safe and easy are not LOVE, because it's not growthful. Easy is short term and can be initially fun and exciting, but we'll soon we get bored with the lack of stimulation and room to grow, so we'll end up creating drama to make it more entertaining!

It's ease we need to seek, not easy...

Ease is about being in the right place at the right time for you and relaxing into it. It comes from keeping an eye out for the right conditions and building our fitness and confidence in the meantime so that we can handle it when it comes and not miss out.

Love is like the perfect wave and all we have to do is when we see the opportunity arise is paddle into, commit and jump up and ride it all the way where it is taking us; to our right relationship! So are you ready to get back out into the waves of love and give surfing another go?

Chapter 18:
13 Mistakes Of Dating Without Love

You're an intelligent, educated person, but when it comes to dating and relationships often we're totally unaware that we are self-sabotaging our chances with choices and behaviour that lack in love.

So I've put together 13 dating mistakes that we all can make. We can all get carried away and throw caution to the wind when it comes to dating and especially sex because it's fun and we want it; ideally now! Other times we don't let go enough and miss out, but that's all part of the learning curve.

However, if we're using the same behaviour and making the same choices we did in our teens and twenties and it's not working and doesn't match our needs for something more meaningful and lasting, we've got a problem!

It doesn't matter how many you recognise, don't beat yourself up, they can all stop being repeated to change the way you're approaching love, dating and relationships so that it is more in line with the results you want and long term success.

1) Unnecessary Vulnerability

Would you give your bank details to a complete stranger?

This may seem like a really odd question and, of course, you wouldn't, because it's just common sense. The potential risks of being screwed over are pretty high!

When we're young we are taught not to talk to strangers, but as adults, there's a social norm to think the best way to find our perfect relationship is by jumping into bed with them!

Even if we communicate for a few hours or over a few dates and texts, new people are still relative strangers so why would you consider, not only showing your most intimate physical parts but allowing them to play with them — would you let them play with your finances?

I'm not saying everyone is out to get you, but it's common sense to be a bit more cautious and make such choices with a sane, sober mind, as you would with any other big decision in your life — or do you not think sharing your most valuable intimate assets, as a big decision?

It's totally counter-intuitive to our animal instincts to mate like this, because of the lack of information. If they're firstly safe, secondly trustworthy and thirdly worthy of being not just in your life, but up close and personal.

It's a well- known fact that the best sex always comes from trust and trust is earned, which is hard from someone you barely know, no matter how good you think your instinct is. So why not use a little more of your intellect, as well as your instinct to assess the risks and potential long term benefits!

2) Good Packaging

Would you buy a brand new laptop based on how pretty the packaging is?

There's some pretty good looking equipment out there and it would be tempting, but rash to do so with no idea how it works, it benefits, functionality and performance. Above all is it worth the value of the large amount of money you would be handing over to live up to your needs, as well as your immediate desires.

Well, the same goes for dating. Why invest a lot of your time, energy and often money on someone just because the package looks attractive? It's no reflection on who they are, how they think, what kind of character they have and what they believe, or don't believe in etc and it's definitely no clue to how they perform in their own life, let alone a relationship.

Of course, admire the packaging, but eventually, you're going to want to rip that off and actually get down to whether there's any substance and can stand the test of time!

3) Communication Confusion

If asked to broker the negotiations of an international peace treaty - would you do it via text, email or a chat app?

I sincerely hope not! We've become lazy, or perhaps fearful with our communication and would like to assume that 146 characters or emoticons can create a romantic connection, with a huge amount of emphasis placed on an 'X' on the end of a message or not.

Chat apps and text messages are simply the modern version of a telegram. Short, brief and great for telling directions, jokes, unemotional information, but try to discuss anything of weight, gravitas, or emotional importance and you're asking for confusion.

Communication is the foundation of all human relationships. Not simply because of words, but it is the tone, the emphasis, the body language, the eye contact and the emotional energy behind it which bound it together and translate what you intend and mean something to the listener!

So if you want to make an impact, be valued, felt and above all remembered then place importance on your communication skills (which includes listening) - because the only real way you can create that personal connection, is in person!

4) Drunk At The Interview

Would you show up drunk to the interview of your dream job?

Well if you did the likelihood is that they'd smell the booze and send you away! If they can't smell it, they would see you were inebriated and assume you're not responsible and send you away! Or get the impression that you don't give a f**k, don't respect yourself, the opportunity, or them and so they would send you away

Dating is just a series of interviews to find the right match. The only difference is you are both interviewer and interviewee, which puts the pressure on, so why add to it by making it harder to be a little objective when fuelled with alcohol where it so much easier to get carried away, especially if the physical attraction is high.

Like anywhere in life you can be sure to meet people who will be more than happy to have a free ride if it's on offer, but those who are seeking value and are ready for a healthy lasting relationship will simply send you away!

5) Exposing Yourself

Would you go to the grocery store, the post office or the office in your underwear?

Unlikely, unless you have a particular fetish where you want to feel over-exposed in a public place, or have a desire for being arrested. Showing off 'the goods', exposing as much flesh as possible in bars, clubs or parties, online, photos and through sexting, are still public places?

The way we behave is like a sales window for the store that is you, and it tells the world how you value what you have to offer and the type of browsers, or buyers you get will reflect how you've been displaying in your window - are yours quality sales leads or time wasters?

Tell the whole world or discuss with someone you've only just met your innermost thoughts, feelings and experiences and you will be emotionally overexposing and feeling vulnerable.

'Less is more' applies even more in our ever changing world - that's not less clothing, but less exposure. Give less away and tone it all down and you will create a bit of mystery, so that people can be curious about finding out more about you and use their imagination!

6) Fast Food Or Healthy

Would you want take-out food every night?

If the answer is yes, then this book might not be right for you. However, if you don't mind occasionally enjoying the delights of a drive-through, or take out then that's ok - you can stay!

In dating and relationships, we all like the delights of a "good quickie" and when you have children it can become a necessity to a) to avoid being interrupted b) be awake and present c) give it a bit of spice to keep the connection alive!

However, if you're regularly attracting and/or going out to pick up the fast-food equivalent in your dating, then you're going to be just as emotionally and physically satisfied as you would be nutritionally. Healthy dating brings with it a well -balanced diet of affection, conversation, laughter, connection, fun, excitement and hopefully love.

Once we have found a relationship that brings this level of substance, then you can thoroughly enjoy shifting the desire between the surprise 'fast food delivery' and taking your time at the long meal out....

7) Over Indulging

If I paid for you to go to an 'all you can eat' buffet would you eat so much that your stomach hurt?

Possibly, but if I took you back there the next night would you do the same thing again? Maybe, but if we repeated it, again and again, you'd soon adjust to only eating what you liked the most and the right amount for you.

When we're first let loose with our sexuality as teenagers, after we've got over the initial experience, we usually rush and begin to gorge. We want more and more of the feeling of power. We play out being naughty and nice, dirty and timid, dominating and submissive, kinky and vanilla.

This is all part of the journey of exploring our sexuality. Well, the world is the most wonderful gigantic buffet of men and women of all shapes, sizes, colours, smells and tastes!

As adults, we have the freedom to try as many people as we want and experiment with all kinds of weird and wonderful things, but even if we gave ourselves free rein over time our desire will wane and we will naturally lose interest because we've done it all, seen it all, over indulged and got bored and feel pretty shitty; like we've eaten too much rich food!

Sexuality without sensuality is uncontrolled and gluttonous and sensuality can only exist with self-control! It's our capacity to play with self-control which creates the anticipation and temptation which ignites out imagination, because true desire starts in the mind and excites our bodies!

Without it, it all ends up as the same old, same old, because no matter what we do to hide the fact - human bodies are just not that different from each other!

As we get older we begin to learn that only love transforms sex into something not just new and shiny, but richer, as we manage to hold our self-control longer enough to allow the friction between desire and emotional connection to become not only electric, but like a live volcano - unstoppable!

8) Trying Before You Buy

If you went to buy a Ferrari you would expect a test drive to mean you taking it home, putting it in your garage, driving it for a 5-hour spin before you decided to buy?

There is a big difference between having a taster - teaser experience to entice you and getting a slight feel of the goods to build your anticipation before you've committed, and taking the piss.

Try someone on for size completely sexually and emotionally (see #5) before you've even begun to date, and there's little to entice to keep going back for more. Or start dating and rush for too much, too soon [See #12] and the passion and interest will wane super-fast or burn out completely!

Driving a Ferrari is fun, but keep driving it and it soon becomes more normal every day - then the real fun comes from it being yours, not just for a quick ride!

Try the goods before you fully commit or get married - that makes sense, but not before you've even got the relationship going anywhere. So why not just enjoy a test drive --there are many small enticing, erotic stages before we get to naked, let alone when we are! - that all counts as part of a SEX life!

9) Full Access Pass

If you bought a ticket to go to watch a band, does that mean you now have access to be on stage?

No of course not, because one does not equal the other. A ticket to enjoy a gig does not mean you're the gig! So why would having sex with someone you've just met or over a couple of dates mean you have a relationship?

Sex is sex! It's pleasurable, fun, great stress relief and just like going to gig it has a high potential for a good time to be had by all. Your endorphins increase, you feel great, sweaty and relaxed, just like you've partied to some great tunes! That's the magic of chemistry, but it does not create the intimacy of an emotional connection that is needed for a relationship, only friendship can do that!

Start with sex and it's hard work for the relationship to match the physical connection, so there's a lot of tussling to make the connection catch up and grow. If instead we start by focusing on creating a friendship to allow the emotional connection to develop, whilst slowing building up the physical touch, great sex becomes a natural extension. So that instead of buying tickets to the gig, we can rock it out as a member of the band…

10) There's The Door

Would you keep going back to a restaurant that gives terrible service even if it was your favourite type of food?

Even if we gave them a second or even a third chance we would begin to get fed up by the poor experience and value for money and so it would be common sense to find somewhere else.

Dating is like going to a restaurant and you want a good all-round experience! You've got to give good service and receive it.

Every subsequent date is an opportunity to see if the other person is consistent in their behaviour if they start out as great and then begin to show their ass with delays, rudeness and weak characteristics, or do they continue giving the kind of service you like!

It would be common sense to allow enough time to see if any inconsistencies are permanent or just an off day, so never deny a second chance, but if your alarms bells go off after second, third or fourth chances you have a choice to show them the door or not?

Remember though they have the right too, to show you the door, so make sure you're giving your best service!

11) What's The Reward?

If I offered you a deal that for a million all you had to do was be with me for 6 months - would you take it?

So far it sounds like an OK deal? What if I then told you I would be inconsistent, nag, avoidant, whinny, stroppy, demanding, picky and generally an all-round pain in the arse for the next 6 months, would you still be interested?

It is clear that this deal is too risky. Not only would the investment of your time and energy out-weigh the potential million, and that is how it is in relationships. In the end, with this kind of untrustworthy behaviour it would be likely I would change the deal midway, pull out or not pay up at all!

How many times in a relationship have you put up with this kind of unacceptable behaviour from an another adult towards you and themselves in the vain hope of a possible reward of love or sex?

When we invest too much too soon in a person we tend to end up sticking it out, hoping it will come good, no matter how they behave towards us. We devalue ourselves for the vague possibility of something with even less value from the other person!

If instead, we take things slowly with small increments of investment of time and energy into a relationship we can have our eyes wide open to see if this is a viable investment and with acceptable returns - and ideally high rewards, for less input.

12) The Space Invader

If you made a new friend who you really enjoyed being with, would you expect to spend every waking hour with them?

It's commons sense that as adults they have jobs, hobbies, activities, other friends, family, maybe children and generally a whole life that happens without you and is what makes them interesting. So why should it be any different with someone you're dating, or in a relationship with?

We all need space to breathe, think, exist as an independent person our own life so that we have something to bring to an intimate relationship. For love and passion to have a chance, we also need space to miss, long for and get excited to build anticipation for connection and desire, so allow space- not just physical distance, but cut out the endless text messages, chat apps and phone calls.

Give and expect quality time and communication, not quantity! How would you know how someone feels about you if you're always there - give them the space to show you if they're worth investing in?

3) Practice Not Perfection

If I asked you to learn to the piano from scratch, would you expect to be able to play Beethoven perfectly next week?

Unless you are a naturally gifted master, like any skill it takes a lot of practice, time, understanding and mistakes to get it OK and then, even more, to become good at it. Dating and relationships are as skill, so forgive yourself for having made any of these 13 mistakes and probably many more in the past.

When we don't forgive ourselves, we hold other people at unobtainable high standards which causes nothing, but disappointment. No one is perfect and along the way it is our job to learn the difference between trial and error, practice makes perfect, humanness and basic unacceptable behaviour. Then practice accordingly by walking away, or watching and waiting, forgiving and giving another chance.

Remember it all comes down to demonstrating and expecting RESPECT

Chapter 19:
I Matter, You Matter, We Matter

This chapter is a little technical. I've done my best to simplify it and you've already been looking at it in different ways in the first section, but a little bit of theory will give you a clearer understanding of the human development we are designed to go through to lead us towards lasting abundant love-based relationships.

There are three phases and we have an initial experience of the first when we are small. Then we will keep revisiting them as we mature and interact with more and more people, gradually creating, building and destroying/break-down, rebuilding ourselves and then different sections of our lives over and over, adjusting as we go along. Until we finally feel happy and content with our authentic self, the different aspects of our life and the relationships we have and want to maintain.

The length of time we spend in each phase is very individual and there is no right or wrong, it just depends on the kind of childhood we started with and the experiences we've had. This of not just affected by our parental experience, but by wider family, schools, culture, money, housing, friends, religion and country we live in etc.

If we imagined our journeys through life very simply for a moment as a scale from -10 to +10. Someone who starts at the ideal neutral point of 0 and then has the secure childhood they are likely to have a natural progression to 10.

However, someone who has started with a deficit of - 3, or -5, or even -10 has got a lot further to go and a lot more to catch up on, like merging from a side road onto a motorway (highway).

I'm not sure that in our current western world that there are many people who get to start at neutral zero. However, once we get back in alignment with this innate development, the flow of energy (love) and have the right tools, then the body/mind etc. will catch up quickly and we can begin to progress smoothly.

First Phase: You Matter - The Idol
Child Development

When we're born, we are the world and everything around us, as we are the only thing we can truly perceive. Gradually we become aware of those who take care of us, to our world perception expands and then we begin to swing from being omnipotent to being aware on some level that *'YOU MATTER, you are my world, because I need you to provide and take care of me.'*

We will begin our journey of adapting to the response of the parent/carer to our needs and crying, smiling etc. to get our needs met most effectively. In the first 8 years, we will swing between idolising one parent/gender (hero) and rejecting the other (monster), as we work out the difference between the masculine and feminine and that we can both love and hate the same person.

Please be aware that this is all very healthy, natural and unconscious, no matter what our childhood environment. Our brains are highly malleable in the first 6 years of our lives as we use predominantly the right side of our brain, so there is little conscious thought, just biology, however, our bodies and unconscious mind will remember and continue to act based on this programming, like a computer hard drive.

Healing Through Adult Relationships

This is why we keep repeating this phase and behaviour of idolising and seeking to be idolised in intimate relationships and friendships, to replay and repair old emotional wounds from this initial experience and fill in the gaps in our development and gain new information to progress.

Often it will feel like we are acting intuitively, but in hindsight we will be able to see similarities and repetitive patterns. We don't need to get stuck in the past, but these replays do give us the opportunity to reprogram parts of the hard drive of our brains and heal muscle memory and move on.

We will seek co-dependent relationships to play out parent/nurturer/provider/worshipper role and idolise the other. Or seek to be the idol and return to being omnipotent. In either position, we are fixated on other people and their opinions, beliefs and validation and will do anything to try to be wanted, because our inner fear that *'if am not wanted, I don't fit in/belong' I will be rejected, forgotten about and die'* feels so real. '

This substitute parental/child relationship dynamic can for a while be a very healing for both people, however, it is not sustainable long term as it will always be outgrown and the relationship will shift into the next phase with a pattern of *'Seek And You Will Not Find What You Need Here'*,

Second Phase: I Matter/Objectifying
Child - Adult Development

Around 5 months old we begin our very slow psychological and physical separation and growth process to becoming an individual, which will continue until it is complete, no matter what the age. However, in puberty, we have a growth spurt and begin to swing into I Matter/Objectifying (this is best defined as the teenage phase)

This phase is messy and full of highs and lows as we are continued to be pushed by internal forces of biology and energy. Now we also begin to push against perceived external barriers of parents, teachers, peers, society, government, police, men, women, boyfriends, girlfriends, husbands and wives, to find our place in the world. To try to take power and have control from perceived enemies to become the hero/heroine. We come to know ourselves, our strength and capabilities as some of those forces push back, or don't move, while some fall away.

It is the normal transition phase not only into physical and sexual maturity, but emotional and psychological. We will feel like Alice in Wonderland, always too big or too small, in a chaotic world.

This phase is selfish, thoughtless and a bit heartless with others and ourselves, we are all objects in our perception to be played with and we will pendulum swing between - *'I matter more, I matter less, you matter more, you matter less'*.

It is massively important though in our full development and growth. However, there is much misunderstanding between the difference of being Selfish and Self-Focused (self-aware, self-caring, self-loving). We will keep revisiting this phase until we accept ourselves completely, who we are and what we think and above all feel and find our equilibrium - 'I Matter and So Can You'

If we feel secure at home we will want to go out into the wider world more and feel great desire to move away from our parents, repeating the phase of idolising our friends/boyfriends/girlfriends and rejecting our parents.

However, if we don't feel secure at home, we will struggle with separation anxiety. Which is normal in young children, but in teenagers and adults, it is the response to not having a secure base in their lives or internally.

Healing Through Relationships

In this phase, our perceptions can naturally shift to focus on how things look, as a way to avoid all the hugely intense emotions we experience during puberty. We will seek to collect relationships and other people, as objects of our desire, like toys to feel powerful and in control - 'THIS IS MINE' and to be perceived as powerful by others.

We will also play out attracting someone to 'collect us as an object' as a sign of the power of how desirable we are, when in fact it comes from an earlier phase — the fear of not being wanted, which equates to rejection and death.

We will become 'knights in shining armour' or 'damsels in distress' and play out games of domination and submission, taking, giving and rejecting of power to practice our boundaries and strength, and we swing between expecting others to live up to our expectations or cut off parts of ourselves to fit—like The Ugly Sisters.

Relationships created in this development phase use the giving and withholding sex as the foundation of the connection. So sex and physical intimacy are used as the power and currency to capture and keep another. The relationship dynamic/game is then dependent on withholding, withdrawing and working hard at sex, to play out being hero, the victim (child) and controller (dominator/baddie)

All of this behaviour is part of our learning to balance both the desire to consume, possess and destroy to demonstrate the power and the desire to love and nurture. So there is a battle between fear and desire, going too far and not enough in our actions and perceptions and only then can we learn what turns us on and off.

It is through these experiences that we learn about what we want, don't want, like, don't like and figure out what's the right fit for us - for our sexual, emotional and physical equal!

Love and loss—connection and separation pummels into us the capacity to have empathy and compassion, so that we become more considerate of our actions and of other people, whilst gaining self-respect to know who we are, no matter what others think or do.

Most of our social education about relationships and dating come from magazines, romantic novels, films, music and soaps etc. which all focus on the 'teenage phase and relationships', because it's full of drama, love triangles and power games, just like Romeo and Juliet, which makes a far more interesting story of intrigue and emotion that captures and excites the audience, but in reality, it's exhausting, unfulfilling to live in and lacking in love, as the focus is on Power!

Relationships founded in this phase are like the moon. Only full, bright and beautiful in a dark sky and only staying for the briefest of moments and then it once again waxes and wanes.

Full of highs and lows, aching and yearning. With so much energy spent placating, parenting, saving and sacrificing — trying and hoping to return the relationship to it's fleeting 'fullness'. Which leaves both people feeling drained, confused and heartbroken in its inconsistency. And once the sun rises the moon soon becomes a faint and fading image against the daylight.

This phase is the training ground, not the main event and will continue until we are ready to stop struggling, proving and striving and allow the sunlight(love) and take full ownership of ourselves psychologically, emotionally, sexually and mentally.

Balance - I Matter, You Matter, We Matter

This phase is the inevitable outcome of the full ownership of LOVE, by loving ourselves and our lives, when we can love and be loved without fear. Where no matter how clear the sky the sun is always hot and radiant, and when storm clouds must temporarily pass through the force of the sun never leaves or dims. It is now that we move between the Sun(love) within ourselves and the sunlight shining in our lives.

It is the 'Happy Ever After' at the end of the drama. It is the powerful hero and heroine at the end of their journey, living in the success of a winner—peaceful, exciting, growthful, abundant, passionate, loving and basically full of joy, laughter and happiness and offers the deep intimate connection we all long for (to heal, to grow, to embrace love).

This level of relationships accepts the LOVE within all of us, that we are all part of LOVE and have the capacity to LOVE. It is the full circle that returns us to unconditional love and loving compassion. Yet also the acceptance that we can love, but not like, and excuse some behaviour in others. The desire of power is no longer fought for, because we know now we have it already, and have become thoughtful of how we wield it like a sword around others and ourselves!

Sex within this 'We Matter' relationship is not the foundation, but the fuel. Love is not born from sex, but in a love-based relationship which is founded on friendship, respect, play and trust — sex and passion are a natural and valued extension at the right time.

Only by learning to love ourselves can we can truly respect, accept and love other people as individuals, for who they are. *'I respect that we are different and the same in part, and equal no matter what* "and so the 'We Matter' connection can exist, and flow between us. If not, we will always return to 'Idolising' phase only seeing other people as objects/substitutes to fill the hole in our development.

"I do my thing and you do your thing.

I am not in this world to live up to your expectations,

And you are not in this world to live up to mine.

You are you, and I am I,

and if by chance we find each other, it's beautiful.

If not, it can't be helped."

(Fritz Perls, 1969)

Not Black Or White

The progression through these phases is not clear cut, with a finishing post. It is like all growth, cyclical, repetitive, gradual and a bit untidy. Flowers on a plant bud and bloom at the same time, they grow in spurts and the same is with us, we can mature physically but not mature emotionally. We can feel super confident and balanced in our careers, but feel completely imbalanced in our intimate relationships.

Don't panic, you will fall in and out of idolising and objectifying and get off balance as its an indicator that you need to make life changes and you're ready for growth.

We cannot live in a constant state of balance because it doesn't exist, every cell in our body is vibrating, although we cannot see it with the naked eye. so we perceive ourselves to be of solid matter. The energy which flows through every cell is always in constant movement with no stationary point., like the ocean's tides flowing in and out. All we can do is learn to move into a feeling of being balanced and know how to return to our equilibrium, with ease, so we don't get stuck off balance and not expanding with love.

Over time using the information, skills and tools in this book you will become increasingly more balanced in the self-focused, self-aware, self-loving - 'I Matter', comfortable with who you are and confident about taking care of yourself. Therefore, able to relax into life, and trust in yourself, love and other people.

You will feel more able to communicate who you are to others in your life and fulfil your desires and negotiate with other people, so you can have the kind of lasting relationship which mirrors the love within you.

Once we have found the capacity for balance, then our practice is living in the ebb and flow of focusing on loving ourselves on our own, and in the presence of someone else in the I Matter. Loving someone else as an equal in the You Matter, and letting go to the love connection of We Matter and the best way is simply to be genuine, honest and in the moment!

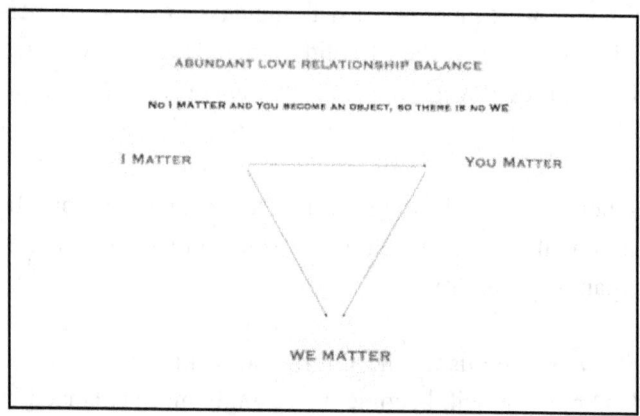

Chapter 20:
Bees Do It, Birds Do It, Lets Fall In Love, But Do You Know How

Everywhere around me, nature is bursting with life. This creative energy is on display, filling the air with excitement, curiosity and desire; to bond and multiply! The plants are sprouting and trees unfurling their leaves, whilst flowers bloom, and birds call out in song! It's a party out there and this life force is calling to our souls, rushing through our DNA and cells to do the same.

It's Only Natural

It's all LOVE baby. The natural world is not constrained by ideals, prejudices or specifics, so this energy of desire to connect and grow can flow freely and unhindered, through each living thing, seeking to create more of itself.

Nature is wonderfully diverse and individual, so some birds and mammals mate as pairs for life; for security, company, a playmate, warmth and that may, or may not include sex and procreation - this is BONDING!

Whilst some don't and have many different sexual partners, simply for procreation. Some stay together most of the time, whilst others separate for months at a time, travel long distances, always to return to their life mate.

We need to bond, but how intimately is up to us. Irrespective of our gender or sexual preference, all that is required by nature and the beautiful energy of life is that we do; by showing off what we've got to offer and moving towards what attracts us!

Why The Struggle To Fall In Love

Sounds simple right? Unfortunately, though, a long time ago the human race caused itself some problems. During our civilization, we got too big for our boots and decided that to be 'civilized' meant we had to be separate and above nature.

We ended up giving ourselves lots of rules and regulations, trying to over-ride the incredible programming and biology of our bodies, which meant we behaved counter-intuitively to what we naturally need to thrive and is now hindering our modern capacity to fall in love, bond with our right mates. We've come to behave as though it's;

a. **Bad To Show Off:** *to show off our real selves, what we've got to offer, who we are and how we feel*

This would be like saying to a flower to stop blooming so brightly, tone it down, don't open your petals and show off your scent, or telling a bird to stop its mating chorus and be quiet! The result is that when we actually feel real emotional attraction to someone we enjoy and want more of, we don't show it and hide it away, with shame, fear and guilt and they have to somehow guess!

b. **Wrong To Be Intimate And Have What We Desire:** *emotionally, physically, mentally, energetically and sexually [Bond]*

A little of something is better than nothing, so we may allow ourselves be able to go for what we don't want, or partially what we do want, but each relationship will be tainted with shame, guilt and fear, and a lot of conflict between what we want and repressing ourselves to fit in and accept something less than what we actually desire!

Love Is Exciting

We all want love, we need love and must share love openly to be healthy, abundant and growthful, but to get it we have to be vulnerable and show how we feel.

As an effect of this historic separation parenting and social conditioning became muddled with fear and control to have conformity, especially with independence, individuality and sexual maturity [the teens]. So many people were educated as children not to show off; told off, held back and made to calm down from being too excited

LOVE is joyful, extremely exciting, makes us curious and very happy!

Excitement is a wonderful combination emotion of enjoyment, risk and desire in response to an external stimulus. It produces a huge amount of energy and chemicals rushing through our bodies, so we feel high! Fully alive and full of joy, it feels so amazing and therefore it is natural to want more!

Instead of having parents and role models who were like good driving instructors, that both keep the pupil safe enough, teach them how to be in charge of the car and encourage confidence and enjoy the freedom, independence of having that power. Many received an experience more like this;

'I don't trust you, but I have to teach you how to drive, as I can't stop you growing up. You can't be trusted behind the wheel, so drive really really slowly, it's dangerous, really concentrate a lot, so you don't make any mistakes and scare/upset me -- and if you do make any mistakes, you've failed, so never try to drive again!'

Resulting in adults who don't trust themselves (their body, sexuality, emotions, desires and mind) not to fuck it up! They don't trust themselves to know and do what's right for them and that they won't cause harm to others, if they try to live their own lives, follow their natural desires and have what they want! so they self-sacrifice their needs to please other people, or not bother at all to conform

How To Get Your Groove On Now

If we want to find our right mate, then we have to learn to challenge, over-ride and let go of this historic programming, be authentic, natural and independent.

Show off who we are, how we feel and what we have to offer, just like the birds and bees!

We need to start using our voices, use our body language and generally making a show when we meet someone we are attracted to. Like the Lion who will strut around showing off his physique, strength and roar, or the Greater Bird of Paradise who does a huge song and dance of feathers, call and colours -- which is all-natural masculine energy!

Masculine Energy Is Active And Flows Out Into the World

The Masculine energy flowing through your body will want you to stand tall, proud, stick out your chest, widen your feet and take up space, make the other laugh with your wit and charm etc., be playful and take action to step up and go for what you want! This Is Showing Off

Feminine Energy Is Receptive, Internal, Emotional, And Attractive

We also need to soften, surrender, trust in ourselves, our bodies and natural instinct and accept the power of LOVE, the energy of life and follow its lead, which is all feminine energy! The Feminine energy flowing through your body is receptive and alluring, it will want you to play with your hair, smile, laugh, gaze twinkly eye contact, touch and accept touch, verbal communication and attuning with the other. This is essential to Bonding!

Whether we are male or female we have both energies, in varying degrees, no matter our sexual preferences. Our bodies use and flow between both energies to flirt and seduce, depending on your make up as an individual, like a dance.

Finding The Right Connection

Only by being authentic can you truly be met by your right mate, so it's essential to learn how to be in your body and trust it! As part of our development into maturity we go through several phases and have many different connections and relationships. They all have important value, but only one creates the lasting abundant intimate relationship and your body will tell you the type of the attraction if you listen;

- A physical connection will come from your underwear...

- A mental connection will come from your head...

- A heart connection from your chest ...

- The right mate LOVE connection intertwines all of these and pulls you forward from your solar plexus -- total attraction, like a magnet - it's the full power of being in the flow of LOVE.

There Is No Failure

There will be times in your life when you've tried to show someone your attraction to them and they either run away, can't handle it, got too intense, freaked out, call you needy etc. -- this is a clear sign that there wasn't enough connection and so they weren't right for you!

Every bird does not find their ideal mate the moment they reach maturity and may not succeed for many years, as one potential bird after another flies away. However, they don't give up and think their useless and unlovable. Instead, in that time they hone their skills for their display of LOVE and art of seduction, so that when the moment comes they can to do it naturally.

The only mistake you may have made was not walking away quick enough or not listening to your instinct beforehand. This is not a failure, it's part of honing your love skills. Maybe you had one or two of the connections, but that wasn't enough! Forgive yourself, once you get more practised in being in your body, when you meet your right mate, you really do know, as the feeling of the full-body magnet becomes stronger and stronger!

My best advice if this way of being is new to you don't rush -- you're a learner driver in this area of your life, so you need to practice to gain confidence in being authentic in your body, to be you and do your thing! Just take your time. You will make more mistakes, it's OK, just adjust, but don't give up, you cannot miss out on LOVE if you're willing to be open and try. With practice you'll soon see when you're being met and able to BOND and can move closer pulled by LOVE!

Chapter 21:
3 Ways To Improve Your Success In Love

Finding love starts with focus; the HOW and the WHERE you are focusing your attention. Focus on the floor and that is where you'll end up.

Often we can get stuck in 'Trying To Get A Relationship', so that instead of getting what we want, we actually become fixated that we don't have one, so that's the result we will continue to have and the cycle continues.

So firstly we need to shift WHERE we are placing our focus...

1) Shifting The Focus Versus Bashing The Sword

Let's think about it this way: I am currently learning how to Fence Sabre. Fencing is a contact sport, so it's all about physical engagement with the aim to hit the opponent.

However, I spent ages only hitting the opponents' sword! Not because I was defending, but because I was focused on the sword as the problem, so I kept attacking it, without the intention of hitting the opponent. If we approach dating, or any level of relationship interaction, or issue with this manner we will be stuck rehashing the past, stuck in the blame and shame, stuck in the striving and struggle of the problem, wasting our time and energy TRYING to bash our way through.

In a relationship 'bashing the sword' can end up being a lot of time trying to think, understand, make sense of the other person or issue in the connection. Whilst in dating *'bashing the sword'* would look like trawling dating sites, apps, events, matchmakers, blind dates etc. to solve that problem.

Instead of focusing on seeking the solution, which in Fencing would be to focus on the space around the sword and the target area of my opponent's upper body, or knocking the sword out of the way and hitting the opponent in one swift move.

In dating finding a way around the problem to the target of the other person, would equate to simply smiling at and starting a conversation with the guy or girl who is in queue next to you in the coffee shop, or standing beside you in the supermarket aisle, or sitting next to you on the bus. Really anywhere in day to day life, simply living!

The world is full of gorgeous people inside and out who are worth getting to know, some for a moment, some for longer, some for forever. Those possibilities can only start though with body language; smiling, eye contact, being relaxed and communication. The best way to do that is to get out of your head and into your body and stop controlling the type of person you want to meet 'like buying a brand of beans' and be open to the potential and experience of who you might meet.

Move away from the one-dimension virtual dating world and engage with the world you actually live in, because relationships are with people. Start by learning how to engage in a normal, friendly and flirty way once more, (without resorting to alcohol). Yes, ok so it may be a little weird and scary at first, but I am not talking about jumping into bed with them or sharing your inner most thoughts and feelings. Just open up to seeing possibilities, testing the waters and discovering interesting connections, instead of focusing on the problem/achievement of 'can I get or a relationship, or not'.

Not everyone will be available to you, but you will find out soon enough if you chat and that's OK. Human beings are supposed to interact with lots of people, even if they are in a relationship.

The worst that happens is you smile and they ignore you. That tells you up front that door is closed, so move on. It's not personal, just a sign of the wrong fit, so don't keep 'bashing the sword' by keep approaching someone who is clearly not interested, or too afraid to engage.

We don't need to fight to find love! The next person you meet might be an open door, or at least slightly ajar.

2) Be Active In Your Action

Now for the HOW. To come back to Fencing I have discovered I have a tendency to stand and wait for my opponent come to me. This behaviour will not enable me to get the advantage to score a point and the same goes in finding relationships. Don't wait for a relationship to show up out of thin air without you having to participate in its creation, or meet it coming the other way.

Love is not one or two dimensional, only to be experienced only in the mind, in theory, or through a book, film or chat screen, but found between three dimensional, energetic (ALIVE) people who need to interact to have a connection and create a bit of chemistry; it's all about physics really.

Love is a connection and all connections are energy and through all living things energy must flow - just like water, otherwise it grows stagnant, becomes blocked and flow dies. So it is that energy must flow freely through us and the best that can happen is to transform it into active kinetic energy. In dating, as with Fencing I must get my feet and body moving and put a bit of energy into it and go out to meet the potential love connection coming in the opposite direction (see #1)

3) Don't Lunge

Let's stay with the HOW -In Fencing how I approach my opponent is essential. I don't just lunge at them over and over, as this would get me nowhere and achieve nothing and so it is in dating and relationships.

The action of lunging should come from being propelled forward by momentum. To do so from stationary over and over would take a lot of hard work and great stress on my body and would have little force behind it and I would soon tire. If I tried to rush and force this action I'm not in charge of my energy and balance, therefore not in charge of the strike of my weapon; so hitting the target would then be based only on sheer pot luck!

Successful fencing, just as with successful dating comes from building momentum moving forward, towards my opponent pushing my advantage and proactively retreating to create more space again to see the way forward for the next attack.

Neither are about destroying the opponent or being defensive, but a dance of push and pull, playing with energetic interaction. A powerful ebb and flow that builds force until the connection reaches climax (see 2) and the target is found.

Don't create hard work for yourself by waiting, lunging, rushing and losing at virtual and often one dimensional ideas of people, instead shift the focus of your dating by playing with the connections with all the people around you day-to-day.

Of course, you can still use these dating apps and sites to give you other possibilities as well and you could just go do something you enjoy, or try a new activity - you never know the potential connections you might meet if your open and willing.

Chapter 22:
18 Essentials To Dating With Love

Successful dating needs certain essential behaviour to enable us to firstly enjoy the process, work out if someone is right for us, if the connection has potential and to give love a chance! Some behaviour is basic and simple, but easily forgotten when we get hooked up with anxiety and desire, others take a little more thought – Here are just 18 essentials, but there are more…

1) Curiosity

Curiosity is a must because dating and relationships are about getting to know another person and so it's important to find out more. However, don't approach this as an interrogation, but a gentle exploration, as though you were travelling a new country. Be curious about their culture, beliefs, ideals and what makes them interesting and attractive or not.

Always aim to be respectful of difference, not judgmental!

2) Self Respect

Bring your self-respect to the date. This links to how you dress and visually present yourself, but is demonstrated in the way you conduct yourself with manners, conversation and behaviour, as regards to how much you value your time, your energy, your company, as well as your relationship with alcohol, drugs and sex. Selfrespect is extremely attractive - long term, for love! Only when we have self-respect, do we really treat other people with respect; even if we don't fancy them or like them, we can still show respect!

It's about being 'quality' and expecting quality in return!

3) Length Of Time

Go with a clear amount of time you're allocating to the date. Getting this right is like cooking: too much time and we can over bake it, too little and it won't have time to heat up (not enough time to create a connection). This one does take practice, but 'always leave them wanting more!' is a good guideline. 1st dates: Up to 1 hour - 1.30 max. 2nd date: can be the same or a little longer. Don't get into the 3- 4 hours until you've spent at least 3-4 dates with someone. Repetition and little and often is far more effective than rushing.

Build up time gradually; you'll feel safer, more relaxed and able to flow with the process and be more excited about seeing them.

4) The Space Between

Always allow for space in between dates, so don't do 'back to back'. Don't text immediately, over and over etc., you have a life that doesn't revolve around them, so live it! The relationship you're looking for is the cherry to your pie, not your whole pie, you and your life and all the elements that make that up are the pie. The more life you have the more you can bring to a relationship, so don't be afraid of space in which to live.

Space stimulates desire and longing, but can also help you maintain perspective to see if someone is the right fit for you.

5) Laughter

Never be afraid to laugh at yourself (kindly), laugh with someone else, make them laugh, be silly. Laughter is key to building healthy relationships and connections, without it relationships become serious, heavy and loses all the energy of play and fun and this so unattractive, mentally, physically and sexually to anyone!

Raise the attraction vibe with laughter.

6) Tell Stories Of Your Life

Share your stories. You've lived, up to this point, you've experienced things, done stuff, met people, have friends, have a career and hopefully are passionate about few interests. Telling stories is about selling who you really are. This is the life I've lived and what makes me — ME! So tell your stories, gradually and over dates; the funny, the exciting, the adventurous, the passionate.

Leave a little time before getting into the dramatic, the sad and potentially painful when you know you can trust someone more!

7) Best Turned Out

Always show up to your date, like it's a 'best turned out' competition. Look your best! Don't aim to look like someone else, but aim to be the best damn version of you! Both men and women notice small things like pressed clothes, clean shoes, a good haircut and, clean teeth. All this shows self-care, but add into that your own personal style and your showing up as a winner! It'll make you feel a lot more confident and capable to handle the date if you're prepared, and you feel top-notch!

Your actions make the statement that this date and our time matters to me, then you can focus on how are they showing up for you!

8) Eye Contact

If you can't look someone else in the eye and learn to hold a gaze, then it's going to be really hard creating a romantic connection. Eye contact is the primary way as humans we communicate from birth. It's the most essential element to any relationship!!! It's the window to our soul and can tell you so much about trust and worthiness of your suitor. You don't have to be in their face and if it's easier to create a little bit more physical distance with a table etc and then look them in the face and then the eyes.

Be brave, take small glances and practice, practice, practice with everyone, until you can be more comfortable with it.

9) Smile

As good as you may look externally in all your finery, none of it will matter if you don't bring your smile, so show off those teeth. Psychologically it communicates 'I'm open, friendly and I don't want to eat you, you can trust me... it resonates with our animal biology! Simply it communicates "I like you, I'm confident in myself and I'm pleased to see you..."

Give it your best shot - Smile!!!

10) Breathe

Don't forget to breathe. When we're excited and nervous our breathing can become a mess, so take control, relax and calm down by breathing - nice long low deep breathes! If you're feeling a little tense also stroke your right palm with your left thumb, massage it or vice a versa and it will soothe you! Never worry about taking timeout mini-breaks by going to the toilet and simply breathing for 5 mins.

The calmer you are, the more relaxed you can be and that's essential!

11) Touch

This one again is about getting the balance right. Touch is a must in the art of seduction. It's part of communicating and building those bridges between you and another and vice a versa. Start small with handshakes, then touch arms, shoulders, hands and then move to hugs and kisses etc. Touch makes us feel safe if we're ready, but too much and forced and it can make others feel oppressed and overwhelmed. Less is more, be gentle and build confidence…

Not touching makes us seems cold, unapproachable and unattractive...

12) Boundaries

Know your personal boundaries. Know who you are, what's truly important to you and your life and what kind of behaviour you expect for someone else and demonstrate it yourself. Never waiver just because someone else is different e.g.: Be polite and show manners if that's what you expect. Say yes to what feels right to you, and say no to what doesn't. Boundaries allow us to be secure in who we are no matter what and know our value — this is incredibly attractive, even if the fit isn't quite right. It's better to know you like the person you go to bed with every night for the whole of your life than alter and waiver for any Tom, Dick or Sally who passes through.

If you want someone to fall in love with you— you have to be you!!!

13) Express And Respond

Have a real genuine response, don't pretend, but be polite and respectful. If they make you laugh – laugh, If you have an opinion say it, even if they believe something different- say it. The difference is the spark of a relationship, but similarity creates bonding if you're not responding authentically then you're not showing up to the date, so how can either of you work out if this is a good fit!

Be REAL…

14) Instinct

Try to focus on your instinct, not your eyes. How do you feel with this person; do you feel safe? Do you like/love who you are and how you feel being around and with them and do you want more of it? It's simple, but it does require you to be relaxed first in yourself so you can then see how you feel in their environment.

Trust how you feel being with them.

15) Don't Judge - See The Person

OK, so how we present ourselves physically says masses about our self-respect and self-love, however, this is not the same as judging someone by their natural physical attributes. More times than not we fall in love with someone for who they are and, usually, that is nothing like the expectations we thought our dream person would look! What's more important: kindness, laughter, sexual attraction, conversation and character, or a hot body, dream job and blue eyes? Maybe a bit of both ...

Give someone a chance to show you who they really are, not just the packaging they come in.

16) Balanced or One-Sided

Is the date a meeting of two people asking questions, being curious, enjoying themselves and sharing their stories, or is the conversation one-sided? If so walk away now! This is a one-way street and it won't become two way no matter how much time and energy you put into it, either as the listener or the speaker!!

One-sided connections equal hard work and lack of abundance in a relationship.

17) Sexual Fizzle

This isn't about whether you have kissed or gone further, but if after the date (not when you've just walked in the door), or over a few dates if there is sexual fizzle - is it increasing, growing, building as you get to be closer to someone and know them. Initial desire comes from our underwear, but real potent sexual attraction comes from the combination of our minds and solar plexus and if it builds enough we will want to express through our bodies.

The right fit will bring more fizzle, the wrong fit will wane, or create drama.

18) Saying No Will Lead To Yes

If the date feels wrong and you're not having a good time, or your instinct is telling you this isn't right for you (give at least 20 mins to get to know someone a little) then be straight, honest and tell that this isn't right for you, put your coat on and leave! Never stay out of seeming rude. Life's too short and you're wasting their time and yours and is fear-based behaviour! When you start saying NO to the wrong things and take action it leads you to be more confident and attractive to the right things, people and relationships you want!

Never seek to PLEASE.

The aim is to find your right relationship where you love yourself in the presence of the other person and love them equally and without need. This love-based connection is abundant, respectful, playful and lasting.

Chapter 23:
Bridging the Divide

Let me introduce you to a different concept to feel more trust in intimate connections with other people.

You might find it easier to trust in unfolding relationships with things such as houses, money, careers and friends, because it is much easier to feel a sense of control. Yet in relationships with lovers, you feel a lack of trust. The behaviour you use in those other places with seeming success, seem to fail in relationships.

So let's talk about bridging the gap in relationships between yourself and other person and why you no longer need to worry about control.

Coming Into Love

Earlier in the book, I introduced you to the healthy dynamic of relationships - I matter, you matter, we matter model. Now we are going to go deeper and explore the LOVE BRIDGE between the couple which fuels the relationship.

Think of the relationship in three parts. One part is yours, one part is the other persons and the third part in the middle is LOVE.

I hope by now you are starting to understand that LOVE is a separate entity to you, as the diagram above shows. It is both the life force that flows through every cell in your body, because you are love, created by love, but LOVE is also something that lows to you and moves through you if you allow it. It also flows around you, as the energy of creation of the air you breathe, the water you drink. It is the universe, the source energy, the God/Goddess, LIFE.

The more that you've built a LOVE relationship with yourself, listening to your heart, developing trust in your body, your mind, your good feelings, your uncomfortable feelings, your GPS system, the more you can feel that connection to nature, to the universe, to everything around you.

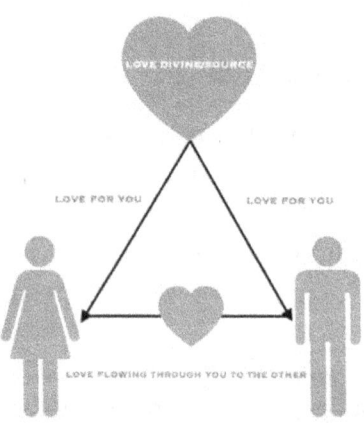

THE 3 WAY LOVE RELATIONSHIP (NOT NECESSARY TO

You have connected to the I Matter and are now open to your conscious relationship with LOVE.

Love Or The Lack Of Love

Throughout this book, you have hopefully started to realise that you attract the people who are on your energetic resonance (your level of Love or Fear vibe) and by nature those who are not falling away. Although they are still free-willed individuals with their own available connection to the universe/LOVE. It is the energy vibration of the Universe and the Law of Attraction that is magnetising you together or apart.

In every relationship, there is either LOVE or a lack of LOVE.

Not because someone does not love you, but because they may not love themselves enough to be a conduit for UNCONDITIONAL LOVE to flow freely, or because you don't.

As I've mentioned on this journey, there are times when we connect with others who show us an emotional/belief blockage (or a pattern of behaviour) to LOVE flowing freely that we need to release that bring us more in alignment and experience greater LOVE. Therefore LOVEs gift is to show you the level of relationship you are at and willing to currently accept.

Each Lover Led The Way Back To Love

Honestly intimate relationships have been my biggest area of growth and discovery to understand LOVE and myself.

1) My first love showed me joy, fun and the purity of love & sex. He offered refuge and support when my home life was a mess. I was 17 and it was wonderful. He showed me this 3-way relationship of Love at its most natural form. I was open and unafraid and yet he also was moved my life too soon I felt and I felt loss.

2) In my second love and first long term relationship aged 22 I was adored and loved unconditionally. We met when I felt outwardly confident, but inwardly a mess and afraid being vulnerable having gone through serious trauma. He brought me joy and a sense of safety. I got engaged and stayed with him on and off for 5 years, even though louder and louder the truth came out and love receded. He loved me, but I did not love him unconditionally. I had loved feeling safe in being adored and cared for in that power position. When I no longer needed that, the relationship crumbled. Love connected us, but the relationship was founded on teenage power plays and filling needs. I did not love myself unconditionally at this time.

3) My third love aged 32 was passionate and dramatic like being burnt in a fire. I fell headfirst in love unconditionally for him and his greatest gift was to show me how far I disconnected from being open & vulnerable

to LOVE and where I could start to love myself as me; unconditionally. This connection was not safe or loving. Again this was the TEENAGE PHASE of power struggles. It though cracked me open to flow LOVE to me and through me.

4) My fourth love aged 40 was from afar and taught me all about the third party of Love itself and surrender and was an experience of more mature love. A safe testing ground for something new and to practice new skills and trust in LOVE again. It faded with time as LOVE blocked us coming into the relationship, but we both grew from the connection.

Each ONE I loved led me to the ONE who would take me to the next deeper relationship with LOVE, with myself and with another and move through the developmental phases too. LOVE led the way both in and out of these relationships until I was ready to be with the ONE that matched my love of self, open to flowing unconditional love and surrendering control to LOVE.

Love The Third Wheel

As you can see in the diagram there isn't just a YOU and ME making US. This kind of relationship comes with a lack of LOVE and energy flow is limited. We naturally feel fear and anxiety and distrust in relationships like this. We are dependant on the other to reciprocate with exactly the same amount of love expression, like an energy exchange.

It takes a lot of energy, effort and hard work to keep this kind of relationship going, so in time (days, weeks, months and years) it drys up completely as there is no connection to the SOURCE LOVE and resources are not flowing.

A successful LOVE relationship has both people connected individually to LOVE, which creates a circuit, like a flowing and replenishing electrical circuit, flowing self-love. Knowing that the other is not the source of their love but and someone to flow love at unconditionally and receive love from the unconditionally. Both independent and interdependent with LOVE.

Getting Closer In Relationship

If we are wanting to attract and go deeper into a LOVE relationship then it's about going deeper into the relationship with LOVE itself. Deepening TRUST in that connection, because the relationship you seek is the other side of letting go of control to LOVE.

In other parts of your life where you are successful, you are perhaps using control, or maybe you are in trusting, relaxed alignment with LOVE/UNIVERSE/GOD and letting things flow.

The CONTROL route can reap rewards with inanimate objects, but like the lacking relationships, it can become tiring. It takes masculine energy to make things happen. If we align that masculine action with LOVE energy we create FOCUS and we can create magic with ease.

However FOCUS, CONTROL, MAKING THINGS HAPPEN are not skills that work in an intimate LOVE relationship, for either partner. If we act without LOVE fuel end up CONTROLLING or trying to control the other person - passively or dominantly for our own needs.

For example: The concept of having someone who makes always plans and gets things happening in a relationship can be great if they are connected to LOVE and inspired action, without it can become a form of control and inequality. It's a subtle feeling and shift, but has a hugely detrimental impact over time!

If you truly want your equal partner in a secure relationship founded on TRUST and FREEDOM and fuelled by LOVE, filled with joy, and unfolding potential longevity for you both then you have to put down the old skills and move into new skills.

Surrendering up to LOVE your reins of control, leaning into your FEMININE receptive energy and allowing LOVE/GOD/UNIVERSE to make the right decisions and the guide you take inspired action in perfect timing and letting LOVE flow through you. To trust that who comes into your life sometimes short term, sometimes long term will be the ONE leading you to the ONE that finally fits what's right for you as you!

Building The Love Bridge

When we get more rooted into our own relationship with LOVE and trusting the UNIVERSE and ourselves we can let go and allow the gap between us and another person to be bridged without having to do any effort, but just BEING in our own flow.

Its takes all pressure off them as well as yourself, to be something you're not and live to fulfil another person's conditional expectations and own lack of connection.

If you don't have such a strong relationship with the LOVE/UNIVERSE/SOURCE you will not feel much trust for yourself either and then you're going to naturally attract partners who also have difficulty trusting and will be flaky. The bridge between you will be a wobbly, inconsistent bridge that will break down.

What you want is a LOVE bridge that's strong and secure, then do your part and lean into LOVE and give up CONTROL in this. Then the UNIVERSE can bring someone who is attracted by LOVE and the vibe you emanating. If they have their own good secure connection to LOVE themselves it will unfold naturally and with ease, as you will both feel READY enough!

Be sure LOVE though will highlight to you both if there is break in connection with the energy circuit. It is not a failing, but an opportunity to release some old perception and move deeper into trust, faith and love with LOVE.

So if you're starting on you're dating with LOVE process or developing a LOVE based relationship, keep your balance with your self-love - I MATTER focus and then ask place your hand on your heart and ask: **"WHAT DOES LOVE WANT?"** and allow the flow of LOVE to be your guide!

Chapter 24:
Love, Sex & Lovers

I have so wanted to write a chapter on sex and lovers, but how do I talk about it without coming across as judgmental!

It has held me back from tackling one of my favourite subjects because it feels a bit like a struggle in the energy of our society. I have touched on it gently throughout this book, but with this second edition it was chance to focus on and offer a different perception on a small, but integral part of a vast topic!

Sex can be such a wonderful and glorious thing when in alignment with LOVE and self-worth for us to enjoy our own or with a lover.

Yet, as a society, we have so many misconceptions, distorted programmings, shaming, and trauma about sex, sexuality, our bodies, and sexual beings who love pleasure and know sex and sexual desire is at the core of our health needs.

Sex Is A Magnifying Glass

I'll let you an insider secret. As a couples therapist, you learn that one of the best ways to delve into a relationship and see where it is breaking down, or is unbalanced, is to talk about their sex life and individual desires.

It is a magnifying glass to how you see yourself, each other, and how you see intimacy, connection and your perception of love.

Most of all, it highlights whether you have fear of being yourself, losing control, and sharing yourself with another by being vulnerable.

It's not surprising as sex is incredibly physically and ALWAYS emotionally intimate....

Yet somehow our society has done its best to make it a throw-away activity and something you do with anyone you've just met, that you might like the look or smell of. That it's OK to order off the shelf with one swipe, like ordering take out delivery of using another person or be used by them, to satisfy some empty itch!

Or to use it as a tool to assess if you like someone on the first date or first meeting in a bar and decide to have a date! Whilst trying to make that judgement impaired by alcohol or drugs. It's bonkers!

But I had similar experiences in my 20's. How could I have not, when its shown in every movie, TV show, or reality TV. It's hard to not be subtly programmed with the same perceptions when your LOVE is out of alignment, your self worth is on the floor, and you're desperately seeking connection and validation from other people.

It's not your fault if you've been down this path too, but it's your choice now as you reclaim LOVE and put LOVE back into your sex.

What we don't see is the damage this behaviour causes to the individual, their emotional state, self-value, and their ability to trust in themselves and others. As well as the dubious and shaky foundations it creates for a relationship, which will always lead to drama and more pain, as it lacks strong foundations!

But we only learn that through experience.

Sex will always magnify and intensify how the individual feels in and about themselves. So if sex happens without the love of self and LOVE energy flowing through the connection, whether that be out of a relationship or in a long term one, the results are always the same. There's no fuel of love, so you and the connection are left empty and dissatisfied over time.

The Intimacy Of Sex

Sex is wonderfully natural and it's extremely intimate because we have higher consciousness and emotional awareness than other animals.

When you share sexual activities with someone, physically you're exchanging bodily fluids, chemicals, heat, and energy. As a woman, you allowing someone inside of your own body and for a man you're entering into another person, whilst giving part of yourself away. This just blows my mind when I think about what actually happens. It is definitely not something to do lightly without consideration.

Most of all, sex is emotional and everyone who has sex does it for emotion! We exchange and mingle emotional energy with someone else in the process.

Which is like getting in a bath with someone else. If you're both clean, it's all good and fun, but if you share a bath with someone who is covered in mud and you're clean, very soon you'll be muddy too!

That will always have an effect on your state of mental and emotional balance - both positive and negative.

Throughout our journey of sexual maturity, we will have Sex for EMOTIONAL status, EMOTIONAL power, EMOTIONAL connection, or EMOTIONAL expression.

If you're both in alignment with LOVE for yourself and so LOVE flows through you, what you will CREATE together with someone who is also in alignment is more LOVE ENERGY. It is invigorating, energising, uplifting, and healing for the body and soul. It truly deepens the connection.

Whether that sexual moment is a quickie or a long languid romantic affair one warm evening. It's magnificent! The orgasms are glorious. You will feel open like a flower in bloom. Strong and safe, and letting go is not a concern, but very easy!

Yet if you are out of alignment with LOVE, the energy you will exchange is your own personal resources - your own life force!

In that exchange, you will feel and pick up other peoples negative emotional energy as well their positive, and you will come away depleted or even feeling either a bit used, off or dirty. The connection won't last, because it is only chemical and not LOVE based.

Of course, most of us will brush that nagging thought away even though we know that something isn't right and often decide they're not the right person anyway.

Self Exploration

In the discovery of loving ourselves, it really important to explore our own sexuality. To stop looking outside of ourselves, but to look within for our pleasure and connect our sexual energy with LOVE once more, so they work together.

Masturbation/self-pleasure is a wonderful way to allow yourself to surrender into the energy in your own body and it can be incredibly healing of past sexual wound as you learn to allow that energy to pass through you freely. If you have had SIN complexes about touching yourself then this can be a gentle exploration to get to know your own body with compassion and gradually reach enjoyment.

Recommendations:

- I would highly recommend Regena Thomashauer's book 'Pussy: A Reclamation'.
- We can hold trauma and emotional wounding in our genitals and sacral/root chakras, so any form of Reiki healing or kinesiology can really help too.
- You may be interested in exploring OMing Techniques or Tantric techniques on youtube to help you discover new levels of self-pleasure.

1) See Yourself

It is important to see you. So gaze as lovingly as you can on your body and if you need a mirror use it. Do not feed any negative thoughts and judgements, hear them, breathe, and ask LOVE/GOD/THE UNIVERSE out loud in your head to guide you with love. It is best to do this after meditation so you are most relaxed and open.

2) Feel Yourself

This is about knowing what gives you pleasure. It takes exploration and feeling, and I would recommend your skin on skin at first, so close your eyes and breathe and just feel and touch.

Don't seek arousing visions in your imagination - that has its place, but not at this moment, as it is another way of looking outside of yourself for pleasure.

Give TIME for this. Make it a special moment after a bath or with romantic lighting and music. You are your primary LOVER, so set the scene as you would like it to be shared with another.

Don't RUSH and start at the genitals. If a lover did this you would be most disappointed, so close your eyes and stroke your skin around your body, use light fingers tips to caress, explore and breathe. Notice areas that feel more sensitive than others, erogenous zones are not always where you think.

This is not a one-time affair, but something to make time for regularly as you explore your own landscape of LOVE and energy through sex. Every time you experience this it will change, you will begin to notice different parts of your body that feel good, sensitive at different moments.

3) Hear Yourself

It is a highly intimate and delicious thing to know one's own pleasure and you will find riches there that are yours alone and not dependant on another. All you have to do is be brave, trust gently in yourself, allow LOVE energy and freedom to course through you. Follow the impulses to touch, move, and then to speak your words, make noises and set yourself free.

When we approach our own bodies with intentional love and sacredness it intensifies the emotion so if you do reach a natural climax, which is not necessary or important in experiencing the pleasure. You may cry and that is OK and good - let it out! It's a release and LOVE energy healing at its best.

Time To Explore With A Lover

The next stage of this is to share your body with another. I can assure you that once you have taken the time to know and feel yourself, and given yourself pleasure, your confidence will soar and you will become intensely attractive. You will feel your worth and the power of the energy, so you will never go back to using sex as a tool to judge a potential partner or to glue a longer-term relationship together. You will not act towards sex carelessly and unconsciously without LOVE because you've tasted how magnificent it can be and so I can guarantee you won't settle for less.

As you move through the dating with LOVE phases with this book, ebbing and flowing between loving yourself and a connection with another, you will feel when you are ready. Start with kisses, touching, and strokes.

Don't rush. This level of sexual intimacy needs time to align but once it gets going it is HOT HOT HOT. So be patient, kind, and trust yourself!

Above all let LOVE lead the way and great sex will follow naturally!

Chapter 25:
Your Love And Life Assessment Questionnaire

Get to know yourself a bit better. Take your time to fill out this questionnaire and revisit it after you've finished the book, or in a month to reflect on yourself and your life and what you need from a relationship. Be specific, not vague and give you the opportunity to get a little clearer about who you are, what your about and what's important to you from a relationship.

You may find that you still have lower vibration/ teenage relationship beliefs and you are replaying history when you no longer need to repair the past, but instead be open to intimacy and love.

1) I feel happy in an intimate relationship when?

2) I feel valued in male and female friendships when?

3) What six things are most important to you in life?

4) What type of things get you mentally stimulated/ interested or curious?

5) What kind of things get you excited and giddy like a child?

6) What 10 things would you consider as fun to do by yourself and with other people

7) Name 10 things you consider as physically or mentally pleasurable?

8) What did you enjoy doing as a kid?

9) Who and what did you love in your childhood?

10) Your core principles - what do you believe in and is important in your life, the wider world and humanity?

11) What are your 5 essential rules for being in your company and in a relationship with you? - *[what irritates or pisses you off when someone does it? For example: Don't be on the phone, somewhere else, computer etc. - when you're with me - be with me, or don't send me dirty pictures, don't be late etc]*

12) What are your personal relationship no go's and deal breakers *[eg: such as cheating, lying, debt, addiction in any form, abuse, S&M?]*

13) How do you demonstrate love physically through your face, body, touch, eyes and in actions, interest, conversation, care, money?

14) What does love look like *[physically, verbally, actions etc.]* from someone else to you?

15) How do you need love shown to you, so you feel loved, wanted and valued?

16) Rate in the order of importance to you: sex, affection, play/fun, conversation, money, being provided for, gifts, manners, providing, thoughtfulness, socializing, laughter

17) When would you feel these feelings:

>I feel bad when…

>I feel sad when…

>I feel happy when…

>I am mad when …

>I feel scared when…

18) What qualities do you find in someone else that turn you on?

19) What qualities do you find in someone else that turn you off?

20) Be honest and list the five characteristics and behaviour in your parents, carers, grandparents or older siblings (the environment you grew up in) that you liked and disliked.

21) What are your five best characteristics?

22) What are your 3 worst characteristics?

23) In your past significant relationships what characteristics and physicalities turned you on and off about the other person?

24) What do you bring to a relationship - imagine selling yourself like a product and what you can offer - be specific! Why should someone get involved with you?

25) What are your short term goals/desires/ needs over the next in the different areas of your life?

    3 months:

      6 months:

        1 year:

26) What are your long term life goals/desires over the next 5 years?

PART 3: HEALTHY LOVING RELATIONSHIPS

Part Three Introduction: Healthy Loving Relationships

"To love yourself is the truth, to love another is a blessing, to be loved is your reflection"

So far we have covered loving yourself, being open to love and loving another, and how to know who is right for you. Now we enter into allowing yourself to be loved and reflected by someone else intimately.

In this section, we will cover the important ingredients for 'We Matter' so that we can complete the 'I Matter, You Matter, We Matter' balance. Which is the healthy foundation for all relationships, however, we will be focusing on intimate partnerships and building on all the new information and skills you have learnt so far.

We will be exploring the essentials to healthy, loving, love-based relationships and managing the difference between unconditional love and conditional relationships.

We will look at the pitfalls of where relationships fall down and go hot and cold, and how to know if a relationship is right for you or not. We will cover the essentials to successful relationships and why intimacy is an invitation to visit not stay.

We will cover real communication and maintaining relationship passion and sustainability in the busy world, and above all how to allow the love connection between you to flow abundantly and long term.

Although this is the final section of the book, you can always revisit early chapters. As growing, learning and thriving in Love and life is a cyclical process, where we build on knowledge and experience. There is no failure, only opportunities to hone our skills, let go of redundant past information, adjust and adapt, so that we can be more and more in alignment with where we want to be and who we really — LOVE

Chapter 26:
Love Or A Pain Vibration

LOVE gets given the worst publicity in history! It's desired and yet often blamed and rejected for being cold, hard and cruel, for causing pain, suffering and breaking hearts.

As your now aware our perceptions of LOVE are firstly founded on our early demonstrations and experiences, which we then build upon depending on what we seek and our choices, which means we can become a bit confused about LOVE.

The key to success in life, dating and relationships is knowing what VIBE we're putting out, and if that's what we want, because that's what we'll get back! If we really want LOVE and to succeed in finding the lasting intimate relationship we want, then we need to be in line with the right vibe of a LOVE connection!

Confusing Love

LOVE is a high energetic vibration; its full, fat, voluptuous and sometimes a bit spicy; basically totally abundant in all ways!

However due to many confused perceptions Love can become not only misbranded, but misrepresented and wielded like a sword with threats of separation, or raised up as a revered idol who judges and smites no matter how hard we worship or sacrifice for it.

Love The Bargaining Tool

- Behave this way and I will love you, do as your told and I will love you.

- Do something I don't like and I will redraw my love.

- Clean the house and cook my dinner and I will love you.

- Provide for me; money, house etc. and I will love you

- Look the way I want and I will love you

Love the Manipulator

- You're needy and weak for wanting LOVE

- I love you - even when I cheated and slept with someone else, or lied to another and said you didn't exist or matter!

- Never leave me, don't do your own thing, you don't need friends or family or to love for yourself — I love you — isn't that enough?

- I'm bored I need you to entertain me, complete me, fill me, lift me up, make me happy-I love you

- I love you, but don't get too big, don't misbehave, don't say things that I won't agree with, don't be too attractive, don't wear that or dress like this.

It's no wonder we can end up believing LOVE isn't much fun and comes with pain. It's really no surprise then that we don't want to trust in it; anxious if we're good enough, or fearing punishment and rejection, if we are not!

All is not lost, the fact is this isn't LOVE, it's fear. Fear is a much lower, shrinky, tight, chillier vibe, which has some ugly friends called shame and guilt who like to hang out and create some drama!

Why The Love Vibe Feels So Good

So let's not get dragged down by those losers, shake them off and let's go find where the real party is at. LOVE'S vibe feels like a busy summer beach party in Brazil with lots of great tunes to sway your arms in the air and shake your beautiful bootie at.

1) Love Is Fun

Love is bouncy fun energy. Its nature is to play, to create bonds and stimulate our imagination just like small children. To put the innocence, open-hearted and opened mindedness back into our view of life. Full of curiosity and possibilities. It's an exploration of the world and within ourselves and each other as though we are new lands to discover. It's joy, silliness, raunchiness and play - plus the joy of great sex and trust combined!

Share this vibe and it will only get bigger and better!

2) Love Is Laughter

Love is the giggles, the stories, the laughter, the teasing and the play fighting no matter how old we get! It's the letting go and laughing from our bellies. It's the bawdy stories and foolish observations. Laughter creates the friendship and foundation of relationships because it's a natural part of playing and gets us through the tougher part of life!

Laughter raises our vibe even higher!

3) Love Is Flirting

Love is the wonderfulness of flirtation - the art of making someone feel special, wanted and attractive. It's the joy of temptation and anticipation. It is the wagging tail of the jumping bunny, the sassy walk of the lioness or the strong presence of the proud Gorilla. Flirtation can be as rich and intense as Burgundy, or as light and fruity as Pinot. It's in the eyes, the smile, the feel of being the sexiest creature on the planet.

The fire of LOVE [desire] sets you alight, heats you up and pulsates through your veins!

4) Love Is Romance

Love is the romance of grand gestures and the light touch of a thoughtful cup of tea in bed. The breakfast in bed or the flowers just because. The foot rub at the end of the day and the swanky dinner out at a Michelin restaurant. Romance is in the eye of the beholder, not the giver, but giving and receiving is essential to any lover.

Romance raises the vibe of the whole relationship!

5) Love Is Adventure

Love is an exhilarating journey into the unknown, no matter how many times we've met it. No two loves are the same, because no two people are. Love has the risks and pleasures of all travels and without both, there would be no excitement!

The adventure of LOVE is its unknown destination!

6) Love Is Touch

Love is the gentle caress of the face, the hand hold, the stroking of a shoulder, or a hand around a waist. Love is the naked massage and the brushing of hair from a neck. Love is the touch of a lover's fingers on the inner thigh or across the small of your back. It's the touch of one to another that says - hello, I need to touch you, to feel you, to know you, to have you.

Touching says I trust you!

7) Love Is High

Love is like being high on drugs. Its high vibration makes you feel buzzed, alive, awake as never before. It's the rush of natural LOVE drugs, of endorphins and Oxytocin. It's the body's cells speeding up their vibration. It's like the inflating of the balloon until floats high in the sky or the soaring of an eagle!

Love lifts us up!

8) Love Is Strength, Power And Growth

Far from the old lies that LOVE makes you weak and vulnerable -- Love is strong and powerful, although it is invisible to the naked eye! It fills us up to fullest capacity and then continuously flows as we grow! It's the fuel to our life, the air to our lungs and the water to our blood. Its power and strength are that it's both gentle and forceful and yet fluid in nature! It's as the Sun never waning, never shrinking, ever shining.

Love expands us, so we become more, we have more to share and more room to receive!

9) Love Feels Great And A Bit Groovy

Love makes us virile and full of vitality, washed a new, brave, bold and ready for anything! It makes us feel on top of the world, free of the past, forgiving and kind. Love makes the best version of us and no matter what age wonderfully a bit daft!!!

Love makes us full of hope!

10) Love Is Hot, Hot, Hot

Love is like spring and summer all rolled into one! It's warm to the skin and our souls. It ignites our bodies from the inside out with energy, so just like water molecules in the pan of the stove, as they get gradually warm, they expand, get bouncy, and start a party!

LOVE is the energy of life and as we open ourselves and it fills us up, we fall in love with the pure pleasure of it flowing through our bodies, making us feel fully alive. As we connect closer with the right person the connection builds pressure and force, gets hotter, as it weaves its spell!

No matter how much time passes real LOVE only deepens, widens and grows, if it is given the space to be because Love is both the new life of spring and the abundance of full bloom of Summer.

If your past relationships or dating experiences don't match this then you've been hanging out at a lower vibe and therefore are missing out on LOVE. You deserve LOVE and it's your divine right to enjoy it at its absolute best.

Chapter 27:
Why People Blow Hot And Cold

You meet this person and go on a few dates, they seem totally into you, you're enjoying yourself, so naturally you begin to think it has potential. Then out of the blue they start withdrawing, become less available, distant and even cold, leaving you feeling hurt, confused and wondering; *"have I done something wrong?"*

So why do people blow hot and cold? Well, it actually comes down to a little bit of science and once we understand why men and women behave this way we can choose to work with it, or not!

Sharing Your Bed

Sharing your bed and snuggling is heavenly. Remember a time though when you shared a bed with someone and woke up in the middle of the night and the bed didn't seem quite big enough; their on your side, breathing in your ear, limbs wrapped over you, there's no space and now you're heating up.

You kick the covers off your feet, you try to inch to the very edge, breath and do everything to cool down, but it's just not enough! What started out as irritation at being a bit hot and bothered, is now getting you cross and boiling.

You now have several choices; a) wake them up and ask them to move, b) physically push him over, get up change side, or c) just cling to the edge of the bed saying and doing nothing.

Stay put, because you don't want to be rude and upset them and you'll be spending the night awake, bitching in your head, feeling resentful or eventually just getting up, leaving to take some space in the spare room/ the couch or going home to your own bed!

Now think of the bed as your relationship. Firstly, there must be literally room enough for two fully grown adults to relax, stretch out and move around without encroaching on the other. Secondly sharing your personal space is an invitation to visit, not to stay for good. Thirdly we're wholly responsible for our own space and making sure we have enough of what we need. If not then we must do something about it, which means either stepping forward, defending our rights, or stepping back and retreating.

The Hug And Roll Of Relationships

A healthy love relationship is based on the hug and roll; then let's connect and now let's separate - even if we may have touching feet to maintain connection there is still plenty of space.

Think about that moment after amazing passionate, hot sweaty sex – you roll away, not because you hate the other person, but because basically you've worked up a sweat and you need room to breathe and cool down! The same needs to happen in the relationship as a whole!

If we struggle and get anxious with the roll away, then we need to do some personal work because we're not secure in who we are as an individual adult; it's separation anxiety and related to childhood, this is our stuff which they cannot fix.

OVERHEATING - *Too Much Of A Good Thing*

So you've got attraction; the energy between you feels electric and you're buzzing, high and excited. Naturally you want more. Desire kicks in and your focus shifts from you to your perceived source of the good feeling excitement - them!

With this shift of focus onto them, now moves you onto their side of the bed! Actually, though it's not them; the source is actually the connection, the energetic reaction of the two of you together and it definitely takes two to tango!

The energy from both of you causes friction, creating heat. The more time in close contact the more the energy heats up and bubbles like boiling water, and you've got a party going on its simple chemistry. Stay that way, even if you let off some steam without turning down the heat; just like boiling water in a pan, it will inevitably boil over, spilling out and dry up.

Overheating can feel overwhelming and suffocating, like sunstroke, because it registers as a danger to us. So our survival instinct is to withdraw so we can cool down. Instead of taking shade from the sun, or a dip in the pool to cool down, we retreat and take space from the source of heat to self-regulate!

HOT AND COLD - *It's Not All About You!*

Hot and cold behaviour in a relationship is infuriating, but the other person is trying to communicate to you physically something that they can't verbally explain;

"You're too close and the connection between us is too much for me. I'm literally too damn hot!"

The more emotionally secure we are as individuals, the more experience we've had with the warmth of other people and loving relationships. If we've had a close, loving, affectionate family who encouraged us to grow and to be independent, then we've grown up in an environment where we can already handle the heat. We're already acclimatized to the warmer temperatures of loving relationships.

If however we had more distant/cold parents, a lonely childhood or felt smothered, or perhaps are now isolated with empty lives lacking in connection with only work and little social interaction; then we're more accustomed to colder relationship climates and for some Siberia will feel like home.

We all have survival mechanisms which are biologically triggered by fear, which includes running away, shutting down, getting distant, avoiding, as well as getting angry. If we experience too much intimacy, too soon, we can't cope; we panic and our survival behaviour kicks in because; we're afraid of getting burnt!

We can adjust to warmer relationship climates, but it's like relocating across continents, it's easier to do it in stages. There's a big difference between living in Siberia and Brazil and done too quickly, like any form of change and our bodies go into shock! So instead we need to warm up gradually!

Firstly, like emigrating we need to be willing and then patient with the transition; adjust our clothing, eating habits and attitudes and take time to gradually acclimatize to the new temperature and like going indoors for the air-con; make sure to take some space to cool down in between each close interaction.

Secondly, there will also be a culture shock, like with countries with hotter climates, the behaviour of those people used to the warmer temperatures of love, desire and passion, is more open, closer and more physically affectionate and that will take a lot of adjustment to get used to, even if it's what you really want.

What You Can Do

You can't change someone else's experience or reaction, but you can focus on your behaviour. You don't need to fall into a panic, feel unloved, get desperate, analyse or get angry, when they retreat, because it's not about you!

Maybe you rushed a little, we never get it perfectly right and we all move at different speeds, but the more you push; the more you push them away. It's like baking a cake, it's ready, when it's ready, you cant speed it up and if you try to turn up the heat it will burn. They're not ready yet to be in a passionate, loving relationship, really it's not about you! Just step back a little and give them some time and space.

If it's going pear-shaped, take a giant step back and re-balance yourself! Don't close down, get defensive and play games, that's FEAR behaviour. Just intentionally shift your focus back into your life and away from them and give them and you what you both need.

Focus on your health, fitness, friendships, hobbies, career, things that make you happy, so you become once again stable and take the pressure off, as you're not dependent with or without them and you can give them a chance to cool down and feel safe once more. Then you can be open and allow them to come back to you; only if they're worthy of course.

If the connection between you is truly strong, then you'll come back together in time, because that's the power of attraction, energy and LOVE and you can start cooking all over again!

Desire is a powerful seductive drug and we all want to get high. Choose to throw caution to the wind, get carried away and let the force of your passion boil over, out of your control though and you'll end up getting burnt with nothing left of your relationship.

If you want to make this attraction sizzle, but not over boil and dry up, then keep it to short bursts of interaction; just like good sex! Learn to play and enjoy the feeling of sexual attraction, anticipation and building the electrical frisson and intensity between you.

Don't be afraid to not rush. Love and relationships are a dance, not a race, so you need to relax into them. Remember though this sexual dance doesn't create emotional connection, that takes vulnerability, expression, trust and time; so once you've released the pent up energy with sex, your back at square one with cold water that needs reheating.

Emotional connection is what keeps a relationship going, so make sure you've taken time to create a strong enough foundation of connection based on friendship to be laid at the beginning, which you can build on, as you start the dance over and over again and turn up the heat!

Chapter 28:
Confusing Being Serious And Committed With Love

"I want a serious, committed relationship" she stated

"Really, why?" I asked my client

"Well, I want to share my life with someone who's fun, have adventures with, be silly, have great sex."

"That sounds great, but it doesn't sound serious, it sounds like a playmate? - is that what you want?"

"Yes" She replied

"So you don't want a serious relationship then?"

"I want a relationship with a guy who's my equal, I trust and I can share my life with"

"That still doesn't sound the same thing?"

Perceptions Cloud Our Choices

Serious and committed are not the same thing!

Serious is a state of mind! Serious has its place in the world when there is gravity to the situation, such as war, real emergency's and life or death situations. A serious perception is about a need for taking charge, committed to the cause and responding to fear and focused on Survival!

Commitment is the act of being totally focused with your head down on the task in hand, blocking out everything else, including yourself with the intention of working hard on an end goal that you want to go your way!

There is no place for either of these in LOVE and intimate relationships!

Love Relationships Are An Act Of Trust

You can be playful, silly, have a house, job, children, be faithful and be free to be you and do your own thing and be a full partner, married, or a parent, simply because you are in the flow of LOVE. In connection with where you are and who you are with. There can be focus and direction to the flow of the relationship and force of LOVE, without weighing it down with a serious perception and commitment.

Love and connection come from being fully present in the now, being relaxed, owning yourself and desire and believing; even though you can't see how it will turn out. Nothing needs to be committed to, because you trust.

You're there because you want to be, not because you feel you have to, should be or need to be for someone else, out of duty or fear of being alone! Love takes letting go of the outcome and allowing it all to unfold naturally, so it can't co-exist with a seriously committed state of mind; it's impossible like two conflicting energetic forces.

Serious Moments Not Serious Living

All successful long term LOVE relationships have serious moments because death, illness and loss are part of life, but as long as the balance of the relationship is 80% playful, joyful and trusting, then it can ride out those 20% serious moments.

Approach your dating or relationship with serious intention and it will shift off balance and become heavy and stagnant, lacking in fun, flow and freedom. It will feel boring, disappointing and frustrating to be in, with a need to work hard to keep it going.

"So do you want a serious committed relationship?" I asked her again. Her response was simply -- *"HELL NO!"* Of course, we laughed, it sounds ridiculous - who would honestly choose that?

Stick It Out -- No Other Option

The social norm for our parents, grandparents and great grandparent's generations believed that relationships meant settling down, commitment and being serious about it. To be duty-bound and willing to put up with the status-quo -- sticking it out even if you were miserable or people lied and cheated, because they needed to stick together in marriage to survive, due to world events, poverty or ancestral social conditioning as regards to men and women.

This settling meant that individual needs, wants and desires for happiness were ignored and forfeited in the act of self-sacrificing for the sake of staying together and fitting in with society or worse for the children. What started as acts of love and trust were often turned into acts of survival and desperation for fear of being alone and for many relationships turned stagnant or resentful, bitter, sniping and blaming the other person for their misery. Not great role models for Love relationships.

Confuse a 'serious committed relationship' with a trust one and you'll end up feeling overwhelmed, depressed, weighed down, sad, angry and very, very stuck! Your energy will literally SETTLE DOWN - you will become less, instead of more.

My client knew in her heart what she really needs from a relationship for it to add to her life and wellbeing and profit her existence, but she was getting confused with old programming of perceptions and language.

Proving Worthiness

The concept of serious committed relationships is that we need to demonstrate our worthiness to be 'purchased/ collected' by another.

Whether we are male or female we must demonstrate a host of skills of housekeeping, DIY, cooking, laundry, accounts, holding down a full-time job, or having an incredible CV, host perfect dinner parties and look immaculate, fab body and perform great sexual acts and have loads of money, to be the perfect mate worthy of being purchased with commitment.

I'm sure like me you've tried because it was what we've been conditioned to believe that only perfect women and men are lovable — except Love is unconditional and the only thing that's perfect!

In truth, though striving for perfection is not attractive and certainly not sexy. Healthy relationships, at any age - including intimate ones, are simply about play, connection, communication, and bonding; an acceptance for being you and enjoying each other!

A LOVE/TRUST relationship is about real life and acceptance! The messy, uncontrollable, unknown, gritty, passionate, silly and vulnerable, the intimacies and the flaws, the lightness and the shadows of yourself and being loved for being you and vice a versa, even when you are a fool or a pain in the arse!

Knowing What You Really Want

Our lives mirror what we believe about ourselves, the characteristics we reject or possess, what we believe we are worthy of having and our vibration. So the greatest act of love is stopping and taking responsibility for what we believe, choose, value and attract into our lives, because if we're happy, we create happiness around us.

"Insanity is doing the same thing over and over again and expecting different results"

- Albert Einstein

Chapter 29:
Why Communication Is So Much More Than Words

Ever felt so infuriated by someone not listening, or understanding, what you're trying to say?

Words don't always mean we speak the same language and speaking the same language doesn't mean we'll be understood. Communication is like building a bridge across differences by finding our similarities as humans, whether that gap is across nationalities, gender, culture, beliefs or simply individuality. It enables us to feel heard, felt, understood and that we matter in the world.

As I set off driving solo around Italy and France for three months mostly off the beaten track, unable to speak more than four words of Italian and armed with limited schoolgirl French, I was dependent on finding other ways to be understood.

Trying to connect was at times was frustrating, interesting and exciting, but it soon became evident that it was not the verbal language that created connection, but something much deeper and far less tangible. Some of the connections I made with people were extraordinary; although short-lived the impact of those experiences shaped my journey and the memories live on as clearly as though it was yesterday.

Shouting Louder Doesn't Get You Heard

Like most people I've been in a heated argument shouting those infamous words;

"You're not listening to me!" When what I actually meant was *"You don't understand me!"*

Of course, I can't do anything about another person's willingness or physical ability to receive the information I am trying to express, but I can guarantee that in those moments I wasn't communicating clearly either.

Communication is not about simply using words to express our thoughts and feelings. Our focus needs to also be on how we express ourselves with the use of tone, emotional energy, facial expressions, eye contact and body language.

If I shout I'm never going to get heard, the aggressive tone and attacking manner will already put other people off from listening, becomes I feel uncomfortable and even unsafe to be around! I lost control of myself and my emotions, so I've become a fire breathing dragon and, naturally, people want to run away!

Shouting wouldn't have helped on my travels either, firstly the French and Italians are not fans of speaking English, they appreciate you making the effort to speak their language out of respect, even if you get it wrong.

If you don't try, they don't respond! So shouting at them either in their language or mine is not respectful and would have got me nowhere, and I would've been the one to suffer.

Free Expression Is The First Step In Communication; Not The Last

Yes, it's essential to learn to express freely what we think and feel, but that's not the last step in communication skills. We then have to learn how to hone our skills if we want to get our desired result across to another person, like editing and redrafting an article.

When I first write a post or story it is done with total free expression; I get lost in my world and the words pour out of me. I believe I've written some wonderful piece of inspiration and aren't I a marvellous writer; until I reread it the next day.

Firstly, I waffle. Secondly, I repeat myself a lot and the overall result is it's not very succinct! There is little consistency and the piece can fluctuate between being too emotional and unclear, or not emotional enough, so it's dry, cold, technical and soulless. Leave my writing this way and it's unattractive and not engaging to read. If I went around communicating to the people in my life in this manner they would think I was self-congratulating, arrogant, confusing, and not really interested in them, so they would stop listening.

All Life Is An Interaction; Even If It's Just You And The Universe

In my early days of writing, I wrote for a big marketing site, hilariously I was talking about how communication is essential to good relationships and the key to good business, sounds good right? Firstly, it was the wrong audience for me, but the way I put it across it was so dry and boring that barely anyone read it and it certainly didn't resonate enough to get a response. I'd put so much time and effort into it I'd killed it!

So a few years ago I got myself an editor. Although I wanted to improve I would dread receiving her response and it would be quite normal to find me screeching and stomping with a flash reaction to her comments and corrections. I had bad habits, more chutzpah than skill, but she never cruelly or unduly criticised my efforts. She just challenged me by asking all the right questions!

"I don't understand this sentence -- Why are you saying that? -- What were you trying to say there?"

She would paraphrase what she thought I was trying to say, at which point it became crystal clear that she'd not understood me. This process challenged me to express myself better. The essential element was not that she was technically good at her job, but that we were different. If I could make her understand and feel what I was trying to express, then I'm more likely to connect successfully with other people too.

If we were similar and talked the same personal development, spiritual enlightenment, attraction, psychological jargon then we could wax lyrical all in our little club of two and that would be lovely, just like the two teenage girls. Being with people who instantly understand us, or you've spent years getting to know, is like a taking a holiday; good for resting, taking time out and recharging our batteries, which is essential to our health and confidence.

It wouldn't do much good though for improving my writing and my ability to bridge the gap of difference? This is why I paid for her services; her responses irritated me and made me get out of my comfort zone and become a better communicator.

The Quieter You Are The More You'll Be Heard

Now, this may sound like a contradiction, but the most powerful person in the room is the one with a quiet strength about them, who says least and doesn't raise their voice unnecessarily.

As adults when we scream and shout means we've lost control of ourselves, but the opposite is true too. Playing meek and mild is a rejection of our emotional self and can lead to passive-aggressive behaviour. So that even though you're verbally silent, your emotional energy and body language is still expressing everything inappropriately; as though your shadow is shouting and swearing at everyone behind your back.

How is your body expressing your true feelings -- honestly and authentically or are you putting out mixed messages?

Good communication comes from accepting your initial feelings and responses and then being able to sit with them until you can then manage your emotional energy and body language. So there is consistency between how you feel, what you are saying and what you truly mean. Your communication is then concrete to the recipient and has impact; even when it's loving, gentle, kind or firm and challenging; just like writing the final draft!

The key to achieving this is to take a step back, calm down a little and learn to hold yourself even when you're completely fired up (anger or passion) to feel what really matters, so you're not reacting automatically, but consciously, so you can be clear about what you are want to say.

We Must Practice To Improve

I came across a perfect example of how girls learn to communicate as they grow up. This morning I was in the next-door cubicle at the swimming pool to two teenage girls and they chatted continually for twenty minutes. There was a perfect flow of interaction between them as they chatted about what seemed like a thousand different topics which made perfect sense to them, as they laughed and shared themselves. It was a beautiful dance between them as they practised their communication and relationship skills.

If they wanted to communicate with an adult male or boy however they would have to adjust their communication to be slower and clearer with only one or two points, as the men/boys tend to find this fast chatter hectic, as it doesn't make sense to them, this is not sexist or about equality, but about the differences in our brain function.

Men are as emotional as women but naturally designed to communicate more physically than verbal with focus on energy, body language, voice tone and touch and so they are very aware of this in others, especially as little boys. However like all of us, we get conditioned to practice one skill or another and for some men and women it has been to be more emotionally verbal and for others more physically communicative - we need both!

With practice and repetition, everything becomes habit. To improve our communication firstly we have to take the time to listen to ourselves and not be afraid of our own emotions and get to know who we are and what we want, feel and need!

We then can only improve expressing that to other people in our lives, by interacting with other people and trying to communicate. Like going through the editing/redrafting process we must get out of our comfort zone, be fully present and express what we think and feel over and over again, accepting that we will make mistakes of falling short or overdoing it and get rubbed up the wrong way by constructive feedback from new connections and the old relationships in our lives.

Until we discover the sweet spot where we are managing to get the unison between our body language, tone, emotional energy and verbal expression just right that achieve a good enough final product, build the bridge of communication and get understood!

The differences and misunderstandings I've experienced have helped me become not only a better communicator, but I truly believe a better person. Like all relationships it is the equation of those similarities and differences between us which makes the best connections.

Chapter 30:
Why Love Needs Space To Flourish

When we finally meet someone we want to be with, or when we have been with someone a while it can be hard to remember about the importance of Space.

At the beginning of new love, we can become intoxicated, fascinated, overexcited and want to be with them all the time. As a relationship continues we can become complacent and stop seeing the other person as an individual.

Like two trees growing close in the forest if there is not enough room for you both to continually spread your branches and unfurl your leaves the relationship will suffer and can become either suffocating, agitated, dry and lacking in growth.

Space For Expansion

A natural response to a lack of physical, mental, emotional and energetic space is to begin to feel under threat and seek to either compete, believing we're being treated badly, or forgotten and not valued by the other, or we will choose to self-sacrifice and focus on pleasing them and allow them to always to have instead for an easy/quiet life.

Without some SPACE and room to breathe all relationships eventually become uptight and out of balance and LOVE cannot flow with ease and abundance here! The trees in the forest who have strong trunks can grow taller and more expansive and therefore receive more light and with no need to compete!

When we allow SPACE for ourselves to be, in and away from the relationship, by making time and setting boundaries for this, we naturally stop being resistant with giving space or someone else taking it for themselves, because there is no threat.

Own Your Life To Create Relationship Balance

- Do your own thing, have your own thoughts, beliefs and interests. It's OK to be different from one another and essential for passion!

- It's OK to have a whole range of friendships and acquaintances who stimulate your mind and share different interests in your life. It's OK to play with other people!

- It's OK to create your own space to just be and not fill it by doing (mentally or physically), but simply just chilling, unwinding, relaxing and simple pleasure.

This is not about game playing, or being fiercely independent, but about knowing where you and another person begins and end.

Recognise the importance of bringing something to the relationship by living your individual life, so that every time you return together (whether dating or in a long term relationship) you'll have something interesting to share and talk about with a mutual renewed vigour for the connection and each other; like turning up at a party with a little bit of food, wine and conversation to contribute!

Space Within

Both the lack of space and the allowing of it will always bring repressed emotions and thoughts to the surface, as though we've been squeezed tightly and released for all the unwanted toxins to come out.

Releasing those irritations and big feelings through physical expression from our cells and muscles tissue is absolutely essential creating inner space and peace, so we can be fully present and relaxed in the relationship.

Use a combination of tension and release exercises for mind and body balance suggested in Chapter 4. Take action so that you release and let it go so that all you are left with is space, peace and clarity. Keep returning to what you have learnt in Part One about loving yourself and creating/being in your own space.

Remember the clearer we are mentally, physically and emotionally the easier the energy of love can flow through you and do its thing. Just like unblocking the drain analogy and getting plugged into the electrical circuit for full power, so it can fill you up and then the abundance can flow through you with ease and into your relationship.

Reflecting The Truth

Of course the essence of a lasting intimate relationship is appreciation and desire and the right amount of missing will spark that up, but it's impossible to be missed and appreciated if you're always there, focused on the relationship or the other person.

In time right relationship becomes an extension of our sense of 'HOME', which needs to be valued, loved, taken care of and sometimes left to appreciate the bliss of returning and what you have that suits your needs and like a 'good' home, it must nurture you.

Giving LOVE space to flow can both balance and energise the connection between you, but it can also highlight the truth of any situation, which may be something you know, but are actually avoiding.

LOVE is a powerful mirror! If the relationship or new connection doesn't actually have LOVE at its core, but only sexual attraction, or the fear of being alone, then it will simply intensify this truth to reflect that it's time to make a change and move towards LOVE, whether within yourself or within your life!

Allowing SPACE for yourself, the other and the relationship demonstrates trust in LOVE; whatever the outcome! Love will always fill any SPACE we create (it's the law of physics) and so with it comes expansion within and without into abundance.

If we truly believe in the relationship we are in and love the person we are with and our own lives, then we must be brave and allow SPACE and give the opportunity for it all to flourish, so it can breathe, expand, regenerate and we can continue to have MORE LOVE not less!

Chapter 31:
Closer Friendships And Lovers

So we're getting to the nitty-gritty of how we move into deeper connections with friends and lovers while allowing them to have a deeper connection with us.

It is inevitable since you've been focusing on loving yourself, that the law of attraction will bring new opportunities with people who are in alignment with your higher and more abundant energy. People who resonate with you, more fun, more open, and who open new doors of possibility. They are reflecting your new love of self and relationship with LOVE.

Existing relationships will either upgrade to this new connection and deepen, or they will fall away because you no longer fit together.

We can have many kinds of friends, and the more trusting an open a person you are, the more you have varied people for different experiences of yourself and some for short or long term relationships.

Not everybody needs to be up close and personal. We can have easy friends and connections with people you play with through work or socialising, that you might do clubs with. As you practise staying grounded in who you are and loving yourself you will become naturally more confident in these new opportunities to expand your network of friendships.

Then there are those who you let into your inner circle because it feels good, natural, and easy. People you can develop a more meaningful friendship with. These varying friendship make our lives rich and varied because playmates come in many forms.

Friendship To Lover

Often we can have this quite normal healthy sense of relationships with friendships, but as soon as a move from friendship to an even closer intimate relationship we can start to behave completely differently, even if they (hopefully) had been a close friend first.

Intimate relationships really test our LOVE foundations as to how well we can trust ourselves. Can I trust myself to be myself in your presence, allowing you to be you and me to me? It is the I MATTER, YOU MATTER; WE MATTER balance.

While you date with LOVE you will be practising with the ebb and flow between getting close with someone you are attracted to and then taking a step back to rebalance yourself to stay connected with who you are, in your heart, your desires, your needs, how you feel good in you.

You know by now you're not looking for somebody else to make you happy and give to you good feelings, because you are the source of your good feelings and interactions with other people are the cherry on your cake, not the cake itself.

When you are connected to LOVE - It's how you feel about you, about them, how you feel in LOVE that's flowing through you to them which is constant and available to you at any time and not dependent on them.

Focus Where You Can Trust

The attention and emotion that a lover gives back to you is delicious and should be enjoyed, but not depended upon, for they can never be your constant source of love and joy because they have their own lives to focus on.

It's like the sun when it's shining bright and warm in the blue skies, we savour it, but we don't get distraught if a cloud comes. When we are connected to our own inner sun of LOVE then we are far less affected by other people being focused elsewhere from us.

Think of it this way, do you get affected if a friend is wrapped up in their life and busy for a while? Do you think that the connection is over or that they hate you etc? Do you feel anxious that you're unloved? You may have done in the past, but you don't now, I'm sure! Instead, you TRUST.

Although we are connected to other people, their behaviour is not in our control and often when we feel distrust in relationships. It's because we are afraid they could disappoint us, let us down, be inconsistent and we cannot control that. Yet it's a fact - people are inconsistent, they can disappoint and make mistakes. It just is.

Instead, we can actually focus where we can have control, where we can have trust, where it is consistent within us and our relationship with LOVE. Then we can let go and allow the relationship to flow naturally.

Getting More Intimate

The more you TRUST yourself in your own balance of your own body, the easier it is to keep your heart open as you move deeper with eye contact, touch, affection, conversations, emotions, and sexual intimacy.

Trusting someone with your body is in equation with trusting in your body. The more you are rooted and grounded into your own body with self LOVE, the more your own sexuality is just something that is part of your body, because it's who you are.

Sexual intimacy is like the deepest squeeze to our LOVE foundations, which is why its best not to rush, but let it unfold naturally to that level of intimacy. Old resistance to LOVE can come up to show you where you are not trusting yourself enough, your body, your mind, your connection to LOVE.

Don't worry though if you've been doing your own LOVE work, as you have, you've been building your own foundations, it will only be a mini wobble for you to ask yourself - "What do I need to do you realign and surrender to LOVE more?", and give your self what you need - you've got the tools!

It's very easy, and normal, to fall off balance a bit when we fall in love with another person, because the energy is hot and intense and because it so magnificent and delicious sharing that energy, but like being a child at Xmas we can get a bit over-excited!

Pacing Yourself

It's natural at this point to want to speed up in the relationship, as you are filled with chemicals, lust, emotion, and energy. Now is when you need to feel your own pace that you're happy with and can trust yourself to stay present. When you were young, you were maybe made to hurry up to fit other people's pacing, by growing up quickly or catching up to older siblings so you didn't learn to trust your capacity to move at your own pace.

I can't tell you how to do it, I've given you the skills and understanding through this book, but now it is about feeling it for yourself. It's like being a new driver who past their test and now is free to find their way. You may start off slow and a few fits and starts but the more you relax the more confident you will become and you will want to speed up.

It's quite normal to want to drive fast. It's fun. The same goes for wanting to move at a pace in your relationship, because when your both in alignment with LOVE it's a high and abundant vibe. Enjoy the unfolding and trust that you have the skills to navigate your journey, maybe not perfectly but you'll better with practise.

Chapter 32:
6 Ways To Keep A Love Connection In A Busy Life

Chatting with a girlfriend the other evening she mentioned how she and her husband had got so busy they seem to have become passing ships in the night, swopping child duties like a tag team and if one or the other had a separate social life it would add to a brewing resentment although encouragement was always given.

This led to talking about the secret to keeping a relationship connection full of LOVE and enjoyment, even when we have busy lives.

When we're not able to give, or receive enough quality attention in a relationship we feel pissed off, resentful, jealous and rejecting of the other, which gradually builds a wall between the two of you.

Healthy relationships don't ever need you to work hard, but it does take a little thought, effort and bravery to build bridges, break down walls, reconnect and be in LOVE once more, if you've allowed it to get out of balance!

Obviously, we must practice prioritising, setting better boundaries with what and who we say yes to and of course make time for the relationship to get our lives and it back in balance. If we can't do that for the person we supposedly LOVE the most in the world, our favourite person and the relationship we desire, then who can do it for?

Here are a few key tips and remember it's for your own benefit as well, because LOVE and a loving relationship is good for our health, wellbeing and all-round happiness!

1) It Takes So Little

Making time is important, but the funny thing is doesn't have to be that much - a healthy relationship can work on 10 quality minutes a day of being close, in person and connecting! Of course, if you want it to truly thrive you'll need to give more time occasionally to truly bond!

2) Quality Not Quantity

It's how we use those 10 mins that counts, not 10 minutes rushing from grabbing breakfast, whilst multi-tasking and distracted — but 10 minutes when there are no phones, no laptops, no TV, no kids, no interruptions! No chores, no discussions on chores etc.… no alcohol either! Just 10 pure minutes to be together and that does not automatically mean SEX!

3) Let Your Body Talk

You don't need to talk in those 10 minutes. Verbal communication is good and has its place to laugh, tease and chat about nothing or something, but actually if you really want to bond you would have more success not talking; just gazing into each other's eyes, hugging, snuggling, stroking, breathing, smelling and kissing! Feel each other instead of seeing. Try to not always do this in bed and without clothes, but when you are up and fully present!

4) When Shall We Meet Again

Aim to connect when you're most awake and not depleted from the day, or the last thing at night, as that behaviour just says you're the last on my list and I haven't got much to offer you.

5) Heat It Up

Yes, as women, we did end up talking about SEX and as I said then, I say now; never underestimate the wonders of a 'quickie' to make someone feel wanted again! It doesn't have to be the Full Monty. Instead, bring a bit of passion into the relationship with a spontaneous snog, grope, or fumble in the cupboard, kitchen, or laundry room! Get hot, heavy, and seek to turn your partner on, but don't go all the way, just enough to spark up the interest and create a desire for more time.

6) Spontaneity

Often when we're busy with careers, children, family etc. we can fall into a routine which kills the play and fun in a relationship and breeds boredom, so we don't want to hang out there! Put a bit of spontaneity into your physical touch, connection and mix it up, aim to surprise your partner - not with fear or anxiety but with play, flirting, teasing and touching and thoughtfulness.

Do these things and, naturally, you'll want to talk to each other again, want to see each other more and feel connected even if you are apart; this is a good start. Then set aside date time; quality, uninterrupted time, doing something playful and with more of the above!

Don't just leave this for holidays or special occasions - LOVE is a special occasion and your relationship needs you to help it along and give time and space for LOVE to do its thing. If though there is resistance or the walls have got too big and solid, then it's time for some heartfelt honesty about what you both want, actually need from the relationship and reassessing whether you are the right fit for each other.

Chapter 33:
8 Essentials For Keeping A Relationship Working

Love is unconditional, relationships aren't!

Relationships are not built with LOVE. LOVE is the spark, the foundation, the thread that binds us and the glue that can keep us together through the difficult times, it isn't a choice or in our control, although we can choose to try to be open or closed to it.

It takes eight other essential ingredients which are in our power to create a relationship that works and is healthy for both people involved and will give Love the best opportunity to flourish, so that it not only works but will last the test of time.

1) Liking

You can love someone, but not LIKE how they behaviour, so you've got to have an attraction to liking and feel safe in their company, as well as liking who you are when you're with them to have a successful relationship. It can be a liking of their vibe, attitude, similarity to you in hobbies, tastes and outlook, or you're interested and attracted to their differences from you and curious to find out more.

Of course, in relationships, we are not always going to like everything about how someone behaves, but it ideally is the 80/20 rule and knowing your relationship deal breakers and that things you find unacceptable and a bit annoying!

It Feels Good To Be You Around Them!

2) Mutual Respect

There is mutual respect between you, that you are different and individual people with different perspectives, beliefs, attitudes, skills and experiences and with all those differences you are still equal.

No More or Less Important Than The Other!

3) Consideration

For a relationship to last and keep working we have to return over and over again to be conscious in the relationship, so you don't assume anything. You both have different points of view, needs and desires as individuals and both are valid. It is both your responsibilities to be aware of that and stay conscious of our own needs and tend to them.

Remember There Are Two People In The Relationship!

4) Touch

Touch is a very important communication between all mammals, including people; it's part of herd bonding behaviour. From babies, we need to touch and be touched in a healthy way, so that we feel connected and therefore safe.

As we grow older touching can range in varying degrees with different relationships from handshaking, cheek kissing and head ruffling to stroking, hugging, hand-holding to more intimate sexualual touching, all of which creates a chemical reaction of body's natural love/happy drugs and calms our nervous system.

Without Physical Touch We Feel Isolated And Lonely!

5) Playful Fun

We're the only mammals who never biologically mature. We're designed to keep adapting and evolving, which we do most effectively through play and curiosity.

Playful interaction can be physical, verbal, active, energetic, silly and makes us laugh, feel great or a little challenged out of our comfort zone - it also includes all forms of sexual play. It makes us relaxed and enables us to be creative and build confidence in problem-solving. We must feel safe enough in our environment, ourselves or our playmate to engage in it.

Play Creates Bonding!

6) Talking And Listening

Not all communication in a relationship is verbal, but we must also talk. No one is a mind reader, so don't expect this. In a close relationship, we might begin to be able to assume what the other person is thinking or feeling, but it's not healthy for adults to do this; only mothers and babies are meant to have that close instinctual connection! To do so creates anxiety and makes the other person invisible and powerless.

In adult relationships, it is the mutual responsibility of both to express clearly, not like a child having lost its dummy, how they feel and think. This comes back to being considerate and conscious in a relationship that you are both adults, but it is something we might need to practice, but it will get easier.

We also have to do our best to give our time to listen and encourage if the other person is trying to express themselves responsibly and not try to fix or control the outcome of what they are saying.

No Mind Reading - Talk!

7) Space

Trees that grow to close together get their roots and branches entangled and die and so do relationships. Two people in the relationship need room to breathe and move and do their own thing.

Even when the two become a family the same principle applies as everyone in the family is still an individual and needs room to just be. So make sure there is an equal amount of space and time taken to be an individual, as there is a couple.

Encouraging Space In a Relationship Demonstrates Trust!

8) Forgiveness

In every relationship, we all make unconscious and conscious mistakes, because we're human. Healthy relationships are based on an 80/20 Rule of success/happiness and getting it right.

Without forgiveness, we gradually build up resentment, stop being loving and create resistance to connection, as a result of the 20%, which builds a wall between ourselves and our loved one.

Forgiveness clears our defences, enables us to choose to be Loving once more, even if we choose not to continue the relationship.

Forgiveness Enables Reconnection

Chapter 34:
The Miraculous Pull And Push Of Love

"I opened my front door and she was standing there with this big smile on her face, holding a home-baked dish in one hand, reaching out for my hand with the other. As our hands and eyes met I remember feeling completely stunned and thinking "I'm going to marry this woman"... It turned out she was my only neighbour for 15 miles in the remote part of Scotland that I'd decided to move to. Having left Oz after 10 years only 6 months earlier, inspired to renovate an old barn. I was 45 and I'd known a lot of women and never believed in marriage, true love or destiny. She had watched the development and waited until the barn was habitable before coming around! We were married 6 months later and I am in love more now than when I met her 10 years ago" Jim

Well, it's our final chapter and the focus is on the mysterious ways of LOVE. These beautiful love stories I've shared are all real and only a couple of the hundreds I have been privileged to hear. We all have the capacity for a deep, mystical, intimate, passionate love relationship with another if we are willing to be guided by Love.

The Push Of Life

From the moment we push our way into the world at birth, we begin our journey to push to have our place in it. We push our way to crawling, walking, and towards and away from our parents — always striving for more. Like a plant pushing its way up through the soil and into the world towards the light.

As we grow up we are pushed this way and that by the energy of life flowing through us and our biological development, and then by our parents. grandparents, teachers and friends etc.

This internal push for life will continue to build force as we mature and push our boundaries going too far and not enough and into careers, accommodation, relationships, until we feel we have truly arrived.

In the teenage relationship phase, we push to connect and collect the next best shiny object and pushing for the next level on the rung of intimacy and sex. We PUSH to make the two parts of equation connect and function over and over, as though pushing to make a jigsaw puzzle piece fit, believing it will make us happy.

PUSH really hard and it will seem like it sticks/fits, but then you will have to keep pushing it back together because without the PULL there is no glue to hold the connection. We may mistake sexual or mental attraction with the PULL of love, but we will soon discover the difference as it will quickly feel like a PUSHING match.

The Pull Of Love

"I had seen him across the room at a self-help seminar abroad. Newly divorced I had got on a plane to attend the conference. We never spoke and I only knew his name, but I felt this pull in my solar plexus like a magnet. So when I got back home I contacted the organisers, got his details and emailed him. Honestly, I felt like I was chasing him, but I couldn't stop myself. We chatted, I got on the plane again and we met. Every time I went to see him I loved it, then as soon as I left I vowed I'd never go again, only to book another flight a week later, like I couldn't break the pull I felt, as though I was being tugged towards him. I had been married for 20 years and was now in my 50's and honestly for the first time I was in LOVE. We've now been together for 10 years."

Sally

Once the growth push begins to subside and we are now on a level of balance and equality in the world, we gradually become more aware of the internal instinctual knowing to 'push to expand' like the petals and leaves unfurling on the plant.

We shift out of living by 'I am here' — trying and hoping to get seen, heard and felt by other people and the world, and move into 'HERE I AM'. This is me. I see me, hear me, feel me and know me. This is who I am and I'm ready to thrive as me.

Our expansion happens in pulses, like breaths in and out, with the ebb and flow of the energy of the world, as we gradually get physically hotter and our energetic vibration raises (inflating like the car tyre or a hot air balloon) ever-increasing, ever abundant, instead of the dramatic and painful waves of struggling to grow, always having then losing.

It is only in this new way of being, content in our bodies and with who we are, can we finally listen, trust and relax, and begin to be aware and feel the ever present PULL of the magnet of Love. Which is always inspiring and guiding us for our ongoing psychological, emotional and spiritual growth to live as LOVE in our greatest joy, well being and happiness in the world.

"What we seek is seeking us!"

In this flow of LOVE we will experience both the PUSH and PULL of desire and attraction, but the difference is ;

1. We first experience being pulled/ attracted/ inspired towards something. This can be firstly with dreams, ideas, visions, or literally seeing a something in the physical that feels like a bright flashing signpost (a job, relationship, a house, but hadn't realised you wanted or needed until now)

like being shown the next stepping stone on your path.

2. The conversation though was actually initiated by LOVE showing you the way for your happiness — not you telling love what you want and pushing to make it happen. Love will keep dropping hints until it comes into your awareness, like little waves rippling on the shore, then building with size.

3. Next, we will feel the push from within (by the flow of love within us), as though the LOVE within us is responding to itself and the sign it has given you. This internal push forward of attraction will get stronger as it wills to meet with itself and connect with the person or job etc you are attracted to — what is exactly right for you at this moment in time.

4. When you're in the flow of the Pull and Push of love it will feel like life is growing and unfolding with ease and there is a feeling of abundance, light and joy, as you ebb and flow towards whats meeting you.

The Pull starts off subtly, like a sense, or knowing, and grows in intensity and this can feel OK with inanimate things like jobs and interests etc. However when you experience it with another person can feel quite breathtaking, unnerving and as intense as being drawn into the

SUN, because there are two poles of energy. It is only in this experience that we feel the full force, magnitude and magnificence of LOVE. It is then obvious that successful, joyful, abundant relationships are made up of two people and a third independent factor that we have no control over - the magnetic force of Love, the glue in the connection that makes it happen and last.

"He walked into the hall in sunglasses and I looked up and saw him and that was it - I just knew I would marry that man! I had only moved to the city 3 days earlier for a new job, knew no one, so I'd decided to attend this class. It turned out we worked at the same company I would be starting at the following week." **Dawn**

One thing you can be sure of though is that this high vibrational PULL and Push of love is also going to bring any last bit of past emotional debris from within you to the surface, that might be blocking its flow. Unlike with jobs or houses in relationships, there are two individual responses and so you are likely to also meet the other person's resistance, anxieties and fears as well, especially if they are not moving at the same pace as you.

It's natural to feel scared and want to resist and delay and that's OK because resistance is part of our human process and there is timing for everything. All that will happen though is that the magnetic energy between you will build force until resistance is futile.

We are not expected to be passive and surrender, like a sheep being led, but instead to take part in an active conversation with love, as we are pulled and pushed towards our greatest happiness. We can do this with simple acceptance and response, or by being aware and engaged.

The best thing we can do is be patient, slow down, steady yourself, take your time to use our new skills to keep balancing and be open, trusting and just go with it and allow it to build momentum naturally. Trust and allow the PULL to be in charge and lead you like a good dance partner and then take action based on any inspiration, without fear or guilt.

Move with the internal PUSH and let go of all anxiety, because this PULL cannot be one-sided as it is a magnetic connection that cannot be broken, ruined, destroyed or denied.

The force and flow of love will guide the way through every growth opportunity to shed any emotional blocks, false beliefs, lies, and illusions if you let it. As it only wants to guide us to have the Love within us fully reflected in a relationship. So whatever happens love at its core and so the destination will always be for you to receive more joy, enjoyment and love, because when love connects with love, it can only create more of itself.

Love Mystery - The Common Factors

Although the true beauty of LOVE is that it is mysterious and beyond our control. I have come to discover that there are a few common factors to these miraculous love stories, no matter how different and unique each experience.

1) The Young At Heart

These stories have never been young love and often from earth-bound men and women, who have experienced a few relationships/marriages. Often the story was told with a combination of embarrassment and awe, as they described feeling like the whole world had conspired for them to meet, and knowing in their core that there was no other option!

I have heard that although many stories of other miraculous, serendipitous meetings from people of all ages, whilst travelling; such as meeting their neighbour back home in the UK walking in the opposite direction on the great wall of China, although they hadn't seen each other for 6 months! Life is stranger than fiction if we are willing to open up to see it.

2) Life Changes

One person in the experience went through a big/huge life change. A shaking up of their whole lives, to get them out of their comfort zone of the old and familiar, not by choice, but some external force that had pushed for change to happen.

3) Instant

One of them knew instantly, like being hit with a lightning bolt of inspiration and showing them the big flashing bright light sign. The other would wake up to it in their presence, although it will feel instant, as though suddenly aware.

"I don't know what happened, I don't think I ever had a choice, it was like force so strong, they say you chase and chase until someone decides to catch you! My wife just bowled me over and I've never been happier" **Tim**

4) Surprise at Appearance

The person they were being pulled towards looked nothing like they had ever been attracted to before or thought they would be, but soon seemed like the most attractive person on the planet, not necessarily just in looks, but in full being attraction, as though being together was the greatest pleasure. Beautiful has been often used, by both men and women to describe the other.

5) Fast-Paced

It happens like it suddenly popped into your life, LOVE at first sight, but in fact, the Universe has been guiding you both together with pulls and pushes this way and that — you just haven't seen it! Once met though it could take a little time for the two to come together as a relationship, as their lives are jiggled to connect and any last emotional debris is cleared, so patience and trust are essential.

6) Tears

Not always, but I have heard a large number of men and women say that once they met the other person, they couldn't stop crying on and off some for weeks and for others months, as the Pull got stronger and they fell more in love. This is the effect of love clearing the emotional debris and opening our heart, minds and souls, especially if we have had a little energy squeeze by connecting with other people. The tears can sometimes be light and joyous and sometimes brief sobs, but they do pass.

7) The Pull

They were all aware of a strange, undeniable physical pull, like a magnet. Unlike sexual attraction, the PULL does not come from your underwear, nor from your mind, or even actually from your heart, although with time it will spread out and fill all those parts of you.

In fact, you will feel it firstly in your solar plexus as though being tugged forward - like being attached to an umbilical cord or drawn by magnetic power. Then it will move into your heart, as you feel love, then your mind, as you grow to truly like and enjoy their company. Then finally your genitals as you are ignited for sexual, passionate attraction.

Acknowledgements

I would like to say a huge thank you every client, who taught me as much in the process. As well those people who have shared their love stories and everyone who entered my life as part of my own discovery and experience of love.

Special thanks to my mum for being my sounding board for my writing and to both of parents for supporting me through all my endeavour, but for being open to healing with love and growing with me.

Thank you to all of my friends and loved ones who have supported my journey through LOVE, helping me finding my voice and sharing this with the world.

Thank you everyone who has helped with the printing and publishing process, you have made it all so easy for me.

Love Jo xx

Also By Jo Warwick

A Life More Travelled ~ From Fear To Adventure

Be guided away from your fear and resistance and embrace the adventure of living each day, with psychologist Jo Warwick, as she translates her funny and poignant reflections on travels around the world, into tools for living harmoniously and successfully with LOVE and the Law Of Attraction.

Available only at amazon.com

**Find out more about Jo Warwick and how she can help you get closer to LOVE…
www.jowarwick.com**

www.ingramcontent.com/pod-product-compliance
Lightning Source LLC
Chambersburg PA
CBHW070534010526
44118CB00012B/1129